Kurt Schindler

Mischa Levitzki

Victoria Boshko

Ernest Bloch

Toccata

Serge Prokofieff

12-I/19.

Josef Lhévinne

Among those present were

Gerald Maas

Rudolph Ganz

One hundred and
seventy nine regards
from Leonard Liebling

Hans Letz

Sasha Votichenko

ARNOLD VOLPE

Bridge Between
Two Musical Worlds

ARNOLD VOLPE

ARNOLD VOLPE

BRIDGE BETWEEN TWO MUSICAL WORLDS

by

MARIE VOLPE

WITH A FOREWORD BY OLIN DOWNES

UNIVERSITY OF MIAMI PRESS
CORAL GABLES, FLORIDA

FIRST PRINTING

Printed in U. S. A. by Parker Art Printing Assn., Coral Gables, Florida

To our children and grandchildren

ACKNOWLEDGEMENTS

My deepest gratitude to those who gave encouragement and help in the preparation of this book:

Olin Downes, Oliver Griswold, Malcolm Ross, Julian Seaman, Bland Bowers, Nedra McNamara, and Paul Berthoud.

CONTENTS

ILLUSTRATIONS

- ILLUSTRATIONS -

FOREWORD

THEY SAY that in the life of every man there is at least one book. In the life of Arnold Volpe there were at least two. The first would be a book typically of the Russia where he was born, in the last part of the nineteenth century, where he knew intense poverty, parental opposition to a musician's career, police surveillance, achievement against enormous odds and, at last, high honors in his profession, in a land where everything was hard for a Jew.

The second book would be just as typically one of America in the ferment of its evolution—its freedom, independence, creative energy and unlimited opportunities for those of all nations, races, creeds who could qualify. Or would it be truer to say that the composite story is most completely American, and in nothing more so than the manner in which the artist immigrant came here, struck his roots into our soil, and contributed so valuably to the development of American culture from his rich experience and background of the high musical traditions of the land of his birth?

The story is told here in simple and unprofessional style by Arnold Volpe's widow, born in the same Russian town of Kovno as her husband, whom she never knew there, but found here, and her life work at his side, in America.

We of America are quick to sympathize with the hardships that confront the youth handicapped by circumstances or prejudice, or both, in seeking a career. Our innate sympathy for the struggler against long odds is a traditional native characteristic. But it is seldom that anyone in this land of the free is faced with as trying conditions as those which confronted young Volpe when he decided, irrevocably, to become a musician. To have to hide in a hamper, on which his friends sat and volubly gabbled while the police searched for him in order to deport him to his home town; later on, to have to tramp three miles each way, to and from the Conservatory, because the Russian equivalent of three cents' carfare for the round trip was beyond his purse; to sleep three in a bed with friends and fellow students, and take turns in sleeping and practicing; to wait agonized hours and days, with little raiment or nourishment, for governmental permission to stay in St. Petersburg and study—these things were merely part and parcel of his early struggles. And it is evident that all these anxieties and distractions, and hardest labor, and shortest commons were only a counterpoint to the inextinguishable joy and sacred enthusiasm in the study of music which led ultimately to close relations with such figures of the Golden Age of Music in Russia as Leopold Auer, Volpe's last violin teacher, Anton Rubinstein and Tschaikowsky. It was Tschaikowsky who took Volpe to his bosom as a trusted young friend, and who first told him of America.

One of Volpe's fellow students, later to become famous, often played to him. He was intuitively recognized by Volpe as an artist of the highest rank. He was Ossip Gabrilowitsch, whose family was in better circumstances than Volpe and extended him warm welcome—and doubtless many a meal.

The Russian associations carried forward significantly into the American picture. There were the Altschuler brothers, whose hard lot Arnold Volpe had shared in his student days. In America, Modest Altschuler was to be found conducting the Russian Symphony Orchestra, which gave so many first performances in New York of historic scores by Rachmaninoff, Scriabine, Rimsky-Korsakov, Ippolitow-Ivanow, etc., and through which Arnold Volpe was able to extend to Gabrilowitsch his first opportunity to conduct an orchestra in this country. It was as a result of this initial appearance that Gabrilowitsch became the conductor of the Detroit Symphony

Orchestra during the twelve most brilliant seasons of its existence.

After graduation from his studies in Russia, after he had won the successive honors of "Free Artist" and "Citizen of Russia" which gave him the right to travel or live where he pleased in that land, Arnold Volpe travelled far—to Johannesburg in South Africa, to London, via countries of Europe, before arriving in America. Here he intended to remain. He had, however, a final obligation to the land of his birth—a condition not unsymbolic of fundamental distinctions between the Old World and the New—which he wished to discharge before seeking American citizenship. In accordance with the Russian law, he had yet to complete his final weeks of military service. He returned to Russia to carry them out. It appears that when the officers in the barracks discovered his musical capacities, they lightened his routine duties as far as possible, and listened delighted to his playing. For it is to be said that the old Russian government, whatever its reactionary or administrative shortcomings, honored and fostered musical talent whenever or wherever it was discovered. Had Volpe, however, remained in Russia to pursue his career, he would have been forced, if he desired to win a prominent position in his art, to become a converted Christian.

The Rubinstein brothers, Auer and a host of other Jews accepted this convention, which existed not only in Russia, but in much of Europe as well, as a condition indispensable to their artistic progress. Offered similar opportunities if he would undergo conversion, Volpe replied that although he placed no great importance upon creed nor dogma, he would not change his religion because he knew it would distress his mother. He said later that he valued all the medals and honors he ever received in Russia less than his acquirement, after the necessary years of domicile and service here, of the papers of an American citizen.

It was less the transformative effect of the American scene

and the opportunities it unfolded than the development of his innate character which caused Volpe, from the time of his arrival in this country, to work with ever-increasing zeal and devotion for the advancement of the young musicians of his adopted land. He saw the great American orchestras manned almost entirely by foreign musicians—a situation which, of course, has entirely changed here since the turn of the century. Volpe, confronted with this obvious imbalance, set out at once to organize musical institutions which should tend to correct the situation.

One after another of organizations which he founded and developed in a series of "firsts," made musical history: the Young Men's Symphony Orchestra in 1902; in 1904 the first Volpe Symphony Orchestra concerts for young professionals; in 1910, the Central Park Orchestra, the first to be assembled under New York auspices; in 1918, the Stadium Concerts, which Volpe conducted for their first two seasons and which became the model and inspiration of like summer concert series of symphonic music in various American cities from coast to coast; and finally the organization of the University of Miami Symphony Orchestra, which has become a representative symphonic ensemble, developing a constantly increasing public and now taking its place under the astute and energetic management of Mrs. Volpe as one of the important symphonic organizations of the land.

Volpe worked passionately for the highest artistic aims. His, too, were the disappointments as well as the accomplishments of the pioneer. Repeatedly, he found himself frustrated by material obstacles, and circumstances which indicate ungenerous and shortsighted actions in various quarters where he had the right to expect support and fair recognition of his accomplishments. There is a bitter note in the record offered herein of the transitions which caused Volpe to retire from conducting the Stadium Concerts in their third season. This left a wound which Volpe carried with him to the grave.

The history of the University of Miami Symphony Orchestra is inextricably associated with the last hours of Arnold Volpe's career. He died almost with his boots on, working to the very last. The story of his final hours, of his insistence upon conducting the performance of the Beethoven Concerto for Szigeti, the soloist with whom he had carefully rehearsed the work and whose wishes he felt that only he, at the moment, knew, is one more example of the man's fidelity to his art and his task. In the middle of the performance he was compelled forever to relinquish the baton. A few days later he passed to his rest. It is not the least of the triumphs of a most industrious and honorable career, with its varied objectives, dreams, accomplishments, reverses and rewards, that he could say that he had done his devoir faithfully and, on the whole, happily and usefully, to the very moment when the summons came to join the immortal caravan.

— *Olin Downes*

Chapter I

KOVNO AND WARSAW—1869-1887

THE LATTER PART of the nineteenth century brought Russia to the foreground in music. In 1861 Anton Rubinstein founded the Imperial St. Petersburg Conservatory of Music. Among the illustrious members were Tschaikowsky, Rimsky-Korsakov, Cui, Balakirev and others. Among the teachers were Anton Rubinstein, Leopold Auer and Soloviev. Imperial patronage provided an unlimited scope for their genius. There were symphony orchestras, opera companies, ballet schools, chamber music of every combination, school orchestras and every opportunity for the student.

What did America have to offer in 1902? It had the New York Philharmonic Orchestra, the Boston Symphony Orchestra, the Chicago Symphony, the Philadelphia Orchestra, and beginnings elsewhere. Theodore Thomas, Anton Seidl, Walter Damrosch, Sam Franko and others were presenting fine orchestral concerts. F. X. Ahrens, at Cooper Union, was providing people of modest means with great music. In chamber music there was the Kneisel Quartet, the de Coppet Quartet, the Russian Trio, and perhaps other private ensembles. Yet no one in the New World gave a thought to the young American generation coming out of the many private studios with no opportunity to utilize what they had learned. The members of all the orchestras were foreigners, foreign-trained. There was no chance of any kind for a young American player, without experience, to be engaged by any of the professional orchestras in New York.

In 1887, a boy of eighteen begged for admission to the Imperial St. Petersburg Conservatory. He had neither money nor pull, but a driving will to become a fine musician. His persistence brought him a scholarship and the opportunity to draw to the fullest from the well of knowledge of the great musicians of Russia. After graduating in 1897, with all honors, he came to the United States for a visit.

America at the turn of the century was a dynamic young giant, understandably more concerned with physical expansion than with the arts. It was inevitable, however, that music, the most universal of the arts, would not remain forever a foreign import, created by Old World composers, played only by those trained in Old World conservatories. Music had its foothold here. What it required was a movement to break down the barriers to professional careers then placed before every ambitious American musician. All this the young Russian visitor was equipped to understand. In Russia he had fought for his musical education against religious barriers. Czarist Russia gave opportunity for careers based on skill alone. Why should not democratic America? Whether or not he foresaw the final results, Arnold Volpe set to work putting his ideas into practice. It may be said that his modest beginnings in training young Americans for symphonic careers eventually forged the link between music in the Old World and the New.

His first venture was the Young Men's Symphony Orchestra of New York. Then came the Volpe Orchestra. Next he furthered the cause of music for the masses when he founded the first successful outdoor orchestra concerts in 1918, the Lewisohn Stadium Concerts. What he had intended as a casual visit to America extended into citizenship and a full life, devoted to realization of the concept he had grasped so clearly, in 1902, in New York.

Arnold Volpe started life July 9, 1869, in Kovno, Russia, a mercantile city of about 50,000 population, on the Nemana and Viliya rivers near the then German border. Kovno was known for progressiveness in general education. Musically, it was still primitive.

Arnold Volpe, aged 3, with mother and father

Arnold at 17

Arnold in Russian uniform, age 21

Arnold at 28

Russian programs

Arnold's father, Lewis Volpe, operated a distillery and was a man of means. Arnold's mother, Ella G. Volpe, was a kind and loving woman, whose entire life was concentrated on her home and her children. There were seven children, six sons and a daughter. Arnold was her first born.

It was a well-supplied home and imbued in full measure with maternal love and understanding. Unfortunately for complete happiness, it lacked an equal degree of paternal understanding. Arnold's father took the role, not of sympathetic patriarch, but of hard taskmaster.

At the first signs of Arnold's musical ability, he filled his son's path with obstacles. Arnold was four years old when he showed his first interest in music. He was discovered trying to play his father's accordion, an instrument almost as big as he was. At this manifestation of precocity, his father was displeased. When Arnold's mother suggested instruction, the elder Volpe said "No!"

It was only a few more years before Arnold communicated his burning ambition to the local bandmaster, who advised a musical education. This the elder Volpe stubbornly refused. But Arnold, nevertheless, could not resist the fascination of music. Everywhere it was played, found Arnold nearby, and at the age of ten he could not stand being merely an observer. He began to try to teach himself to play the violin.

This evidence of unquenchable determination only brought more objections from his father. But his mother could not ignore these signs of special talent. She considered them most admirable and was delighted.

The elder Volpe's severe opposition brought two results he did not expect. Arnold's eagerness to become a musician was thoroughly fired, and coupled with it now was his mother's firm sympathy. She expressed this in action that was vigorous and militantly productive.

Arnold was allowed to take violin lessons from the bandmaster. The boy's talent was at once apparent. Soon, he was playing in the student orchestra at the *gymnasium*. Then he studied the viola and shortly thereafter was playing in quartets. From the beginning, he showed an interest clearly beyond the voice of a single instrument. Often he said, recalling those early years:

"I would run a mile, with my fiddle bouncing on my shoulder, if I thought there was a chance to play sonatas with a pianist. I was simply crazy about ensemble playing."

This special love, not for just a single instrument, but for the music of ensemble playing, developed steadily from the earliest days. By the time he was twelve, he was organizing small bands, orchestras, and choruses—a stripling leader even before he had mastered his violin.

He told his children, years later, of those tender days:

"I would march ahead of all the bands in the parade, conducting. I yearned to play all the instruments. One day I brought home a trumpet. My father forbade it. He couldn't stand the awful noise, he said. So henceforth, I blew it into a pillow. *But I blew it.*

"I was told, in later life, that I was a very quiet and obedient boy in all other ways. But I defied anyone who interfered with my progress in the study of music."

Why was Arnold's father so harsh in opposing a musical career? Perhaps we can discern his reasoning. Although he played the accordion and the violin, it was just for his own pleasure. Having no marked talent nor inclination, the question of a musical career for himself had never arisen.

But he did have a basic conception of a professional career in music. It was limited, unfortunately, to what he knew of musicians in Kovno. What, indeed, was a musician? A simple-minded fellow who stood in the corner at weddings and parties and scraped tunes for the fun of it—or at best for a few kopeks from his betters.

A son of Lewis Volpe be a musician? Hardly! A child was a child, and, of course, must be expected to have childish ambitions. But there was no need for a Volpe to waste his life being a mere musician.

Everywhere in Russia, when a musical career was to be considered in the fullest sense, other factors had to be weighed. Whether the individual had talent was by no means the main question.

The days of Russia under the Czars had their special brands of political, religious and racial bigotry. A Jew of surpassing talent could in Russia succeed in climbing to the heights—Anton Rubinstein, for example. But he was descended from converted ancestors. For a youth of orthodox parents, the heights to be scaled were numerous and steep. The barricades of bigotry rose straight-walled and glowering, against the most formidable ability in the arts. Before them the possession of great talent meant little.

A Jew might make cloth or goods of brass. He might distill beverages. Buyers in the shops did not ask: "Who made this dress, this samovar, this vodka? A Jew?"

No, that they did not ask. But let a youth with a violin offer a concert with a price asked for tickets, what then did they ask? A Jew could not even travel freely in Russia. Nor could he legally leave the country—unless given a privileged permission.

Who could predict, moreover, how long life itself would last? The always smouldering flames of bigotry might leap up in raging pogroms anywhere at any time.

Arnold's mother knew about the looming heights, forbidding barricades and the dangers. But she knew, also, that there were exceptions and by-passes open to one of such talent as her son showed and in these she had great belief.

In the constant battle between Arnold and his father, it became more and more evident that, in addition to his talent, Arnold had other qualities of equal importance—dynamic emotion and fortitude. He applied his dynamic emotion to study and practice, he showed his courage in constantly resisting his father's negation.

Arnold's mother demonstrated that she, too, had emotion and fortitude.

When Arnold had absorbed all that could be taught of music in Kovno, there came the question of where he should go next.

To all suggestions, the elder Volpe was deaf. When tears and persuasions failed, Arnold's mother recognized in the unyielding patriarch's stoniness an absolute impasse. This she solved by adroitly side-stepping.

Off to Warsaw went the mother, the son and his violin.

Arnold's father refused all financial help.

In Warsaw, however, his mother had a cousin, Leon Schavitz. He had eight children, and his house was full, but he was willing to feed another mouth. Arnold's mother left him with them.

In describing his experiences long afterward, Arnold said:

"Jews, without the permission of the Governor, were not allowed to live in Warsaw. My mother and the Schavitzes were all fully aware of the risk they were taking. They knew, too, however, that the neighbors were friendly and would not inform the police of the addition of a fifteen-year-old boy to the household.

"But there was one factor they had not realized. If I were accepted as a scholarship pupil at the Warsaw Musical Institute, which was the intention, the acceptance would also carry with it permission to live in Warsaw!"

On acceptance by the Institute, everything depended.

"So I practiced all day long and sometimes far into the night. This led to trouble. The family was driven almost to despair. But they understood the necessity. Most of the neighbors also had a great sympathy for music and forbore.

"But others were unable to stand the strain of my incessant practicing, and to get rid of me, one reported to the police that a stranger was in the neighborhood.

"Friends immediately heard about this and informed the

Schavitzes. The search for the 'stranger,' everyone knew, would be pursued vigorously. Immediately the violin was hushed. A system of clandestine warnings of the approach of the police was arranged by the Schavitzes.

"For a while, these always enabled them to get the 'stranger' out of the house and hidden in time. Then at 2 a.m., came a surprise knock at the door. We all knew the knock. The police!

"I was put inside a box couch, and the entire family sat nonchalantly on top. Before the police finished their search and left, I almost smothered to death. Such was typical of what went on in Russia."

Soon—and luckily—Arnold was called before Mr. Schultz, concertmaster of the Warsaw Opera Company, who conducted examinations for the Warsaw Musical Institute. There was a scurry to scrape together the three rubles for the examination fee.

Arnold played his entire repertoire and did some sight reading. He was recommended as a "gifted and deserving pupil for a full scholarship." This enabled him to stay at the Institute for three years.

His first teacher was Ostrovsky, an old man but a good teacher. The second year, it was Isidore Lotto, winner of the first prize at the Paris Conservatory. The third year, it was Ignace Freeman, also a celebrity. Makoffski was his teacher in ensemble. Of him, Arnold recalled fervent memories:

"He was very fond of me and often invited me to his home. In one of the cold winters, he insisted on giving me his overcoat, as I had none."

By the end of the first year at the Institute, Arnold's father had relented to the extent of permitting his mother to send fifteen rubles a month—at that time $7.50. Augmenting this a bit with playing and tutoring, Arnold was able to leave the Schavitzes and "branch out" for himself. The "branching out" consisted of taking a room with three other happy and ambitious music students. The room had a piano—but only one bed.

Sometimes the four students alternated in pairs at sleeping and practicing. Sometimes all practiced at once, then all slept. This was considered the least efficient arrangement, for when all slept, three were in the bed, and the unlucky fourth was on the floor under the piano.

The combination considered ideal was three in the bed while the fourth practiced. As musicians, fully understanding the necessity, the practicing of another never disturbed their slumbers.

Another reason Arnold could sleep through anything in those days was the price of the horse-car fare to school—three kopeks (100 kopeks to the ruble). He didn't have it. Daily he walked to his lessons, an hour and a half each way, carrying his fiddle, well-protected in a ten-pound case.

With rare exceptions, meals in the student restaurant at six kopeks were beyond his finances. Mostly his food was tea, rye bread and butter prepared in his room and bought nearly always on credit. So many of the music students existed on credit. A memorable figure in the lives of all of them was the owner of a grocery store, who was sympathetic toward all students of music. He would carry them on credit until the first of each month, when money would come from home. Bills were paid up, then everybody would start all over again—on credit.

Roommates with Arnold in the blissful atmosphere of concentration on music were the Altschuler brothers, who later came to America. Modest Altschuler, the 'cellist, became conductor of the Russian Symphony Orchestra in New York, and Jacob was always considered one of the best viola players in New York.

In Arnold's second year in Warsaw—as if the fates at last had grown softer-hearted toward him—he tasted the joys of little rewards and triumphs. Toward the end of the spring term, he heard musicians were needed to play in a circus. When he applied, the leader auditioned him, then asked his experience.

When Arnold told him only in school orchestras, the leader said it didn't count; he should come to rehearsal for a trial.

"After the first rehearsal, he asked me to play along for experience," Arnold recounted.

"I played for two weeks. When I went to receive my pay, he handed me a ruble and said, 'For strings.' This was my first paid engagement. But six weeks later, when this same leader asked me to play again, I said, 'Oh no! Not for strings. You pay me in advance.'

"He did—three rubles a performance. After the school year was over, he gave me a summer engagement at thirty rubles a week. I began to eat regular meals, occasionally indulging myself with a glass of beer and allowing myself a few other luxuries."

During the last year at the Institute, he made friends with Mrs. Charles Steinberg, the prominent and wealthy first cousin of Ossip Gabrilowitsch. A fine pianist, besides playing ensemble music with talented and ambitious students, she enjoyed helping them. She aided Arnold financially and, upon learning he intended to continue his studies in St. Petersburg, gave him a letter to her sister there.

The most heart-warming aspect of the finale of his three years in Warsaw was not so much the words on his diploma of December 1887—"With marked talent and success"—or his appearance as honored soloist at the commencement concert, or the generous approval of the newspapers for his playing of the *minuet* and *molto perpetuo* from the suite by Raff, but what he discovered with surprise upon arriving home in Kovno.

He found his father had been carrying around the newspaper clippings about his graduation performance. The elder Volpe was displaying them to relatives and friends at every conceivable opportunity. Proudly he acclaimed the prowess of his gifted eighteen-year-old son, admitting Arnold was justified in making music his life work.

Arnold was immediately invited to give a recital in Kovno, which he did.

Years later, he would begin his recollections of the event by saying with a puckish smile: "Overnight I became a celebrity." Then, with a broad, beaming grin, he would add: "At least to my mother—and to my father, who somehow managed to be there."

Chapter II
ST. PETERSBURG — 1887

THE GREAT VIOLINIST, Leopold Auer, became head of the violin department of the Imperial Conservatory of St. Petersburg a year before Arnold Volpe was born. One day in 1887 the eighteen-year-old lad knocked at the door of the Auer home.

Arnold had a letter to Auer from his last teacher in Warsaw.

As in Warsaw, Jews could not live in St. Petersburg without permission of the Governor. Arnold had anticipated the situation.

Before leaving home he asked the Governor of Kovno to send a letter to the Governor of St. Petersburg in care of Professor Auer, recommending that, as a deserving musician, he be permitted to reside there.

"I took my fiddle and called on Professor Auer," he told me of that critical morning. "I received a cold reception. He told me abruptly to take out my violin and play something. Very timidly I asked him what he wished to hear. 'Anything at all,' he said."

Without comment, Auer played Arnold's accompaniments and listened for some time. Suddenly he stopped and said, "You have talent, but how dared you to come here—a Jew without permission.' "

Arnold told him about the letter he had arranged for and asked Auer if it had not come from the Governor.

"No," Auer replied. "Come back when you get the permit."

Surely the letter from Kovno had only been delayed. The next morning Arnold stood on the steps of the Conservatory, waiting for Auer. Every morning for three weeks he stood on the steps, waiting.

"I would tip my hat," Arnold would recall, "and ask, 'Have you heard yet?' "

The answer was always the same. "Not yet."

The chill temperatures were getting lower. The Russian winter was coming on swiftly. Finally Auer's sympathy was so aroused that one morning he said, "Here is a letter to Varshavski. He's an influential banker and music patron, a friend of mine and of the Governor. Go and see him."

Arnold rushed off jubilantly. He presented the letter in person. Varshavski told him he would take care of it as soon as possible.

But another three weeks passed. The mercury kept dropping, snow swirled and piled deeper. Each morning the Volpe-Auer scene on the Conservatory steps was repeated. The tip of the hat. The anxious question. The disappointing reply.

Arnold had no warm coat. He was freezing. One morning, he stopped Professor Auer and through chattering teeth told him he would have to leave. Professor Auer said, "Wait."

He called a sleigh and went personally to see the Governor. When he returned everything had been arranged for Arnold's permission to stay in St. Petersburg.

"I had walked the streets of St. Petersburg for six weeks. Everyone was afraid to harbor a stranger, especially a Jewish boy," Arnold related to me. "My joy now was boundless. On a full scholarship for *four years* I was accepted by Professor Auer—the happiest pupil in the entire Imperial Conservatory of St. Petersburg—although somewhat bewildered."

And indeed might a youth be confused. Who could comprehend the strangeness of Russia? Arnold could only ask questions—and ask them only of himself, for some questions one asked of no one else in Russia.

Most baffling of all, who could answer why the Imperial Government suppressed Jews in so many ways, yet when the red tape was broken, lavished a full, four-year scholarship on Arnold Volpe?

Stranger still, was not the director of the Imperial Conservatory, Anton Rubinstein, albeit converted to Christianity, a Jew?

Could it be that in the great enigmatical soul of Russia a surpassing love of music sometimes overwhelmed all else?

But such imponderables did not long occupy Arnold's thoughts. He was definitely not much interested in matters of politics, ethnology or religion then. Music, music, music filled his brain, crowded his heart. He remembered distinctly how Auer took him to Rubinstein simply with these words, "Here is the boy I spoke to you about."

Rubinstein looked him over searchingly and shook hands, endorsing Auer's acceptance of the new pupil by saying warmly, "I congratulate you, young man."

Now were dreams fulfilled. Now were visions become realities—far, far beyond the most spirited creations of his imagination. Now did he walk with the giants and gods—although humbly. Now did he hear their voices and see their faces, and they accepted and taught him.

He hardly took time to eat or sleep. He worked, worked, worked, propelled by the joy of glorious opportunity, burning with zeal for the new fields to conquer, buoyed and energized by abundant, robust health.

The great Auer placed Arnold for the first year under his first assistant in the violin department, Professor Nicolai Galkin, but naturally under his personal supervision.

His harmony teacher was Professor Anotolii Liadov, whose shyness was proverbial and who hated teaching, but was remarkably fine at it. Rimsky-Korsakov, with whom Liadov collaborated in composing, believed Arnold was in truth most gifted. He took piano from Czerni and history of music from Sacketti. There was also a general academic course.

From these great teachers he received what his soul and flaming ambition sought. Moreover, in St. Petersburg, he was able to support himself by playing in theatre orchestras and by tutoring. But more important, here in the great city, in a way that had never been possible in Warsaw, Arnold found the inspiration of friendships on a new level. Here music was not only on the loftiest professional plane, but constituted the warp and woof of a brilliant and cultured society.

The "open sesame" to it was birth, talent, personality or position. Those older members who belonged by reason of one or sometimes all requirements, however, welcomed gifted young people who showed fine promise.

Arnold entered this circle on several qualifications. During his first year in St. Petersburg, he presented his letter from Mrs. Steinberg of Warsaw to her sister, Mrs. Cohn. Virginia Cohn, her daughter, was an Auer pupil. In her home he met the Gabrilowitsch family, the beginning of rich and intimate friendships lasting down through the years of fully measured sorrows, ovations and great achievements.

Ossip Gabrilowitsch was Arnold's closest classmate at the Conservatory. Although he was seven years younger, he was remarkably mature in music as well as other aspects. On Arnold's first visit to the Gabrilowitsch home, Ossip, then only eleven years old, played for him an entire Beethoven sonata from memory. Many years later, in New York, Ossip demonstrated unusual memory for more than music. He recalled exactly how, after listening to the Beethoven sonata, Arnold had prophesied to him that "if you do not succeed, no one will."

As students they played a great deal of ensemble, often with Ossip's older brother, Arthur, a gifted amateur 'cellist. Ossip's sister, Pauline, was just Arnold's age, and they became very good friends, attested over the years by the letters that went back and forth, keeping the ties, refreshing the memories of those golden days of youth and glorious music in St. Petersburg.

It was Pauline Gabrilowitsch who gave Arnold a treasured keepsake—a lovely, small bronze dachshund. He carried the little bronze dog with him forever after. It was on his desk in his study, on his bedside table when he was ill. As the years passed, it became more than a memento of Pauline Gabrilowitsch and the Gabrilowitsch family; it was a beloved reminder of all the days of his youth—of hard study, of good times, and of inspiration and achievement in St. Petersburg.

It was not only the Gabrilowitsch children who made that home so important to Arnold. Ossip's father was a man of culture and wealth. His presence set the tone of encouragement for art and music. Arnold could not help contrasting his attitude with that of his own father.

In his student days away from home, Mme. Gabrilowitsch became Arnold's St. Petersburg mother.

"She never failed to comfort or feed me," he recounted. "When I would go to her hungry or discouraged, she did not hesitate in discerning which of those young artist's maladies I was suffering from at the moment. She could read my moods, my needs, just like her Ossip's."

The serene, yet culturally busy pattern of the Gabrilowitsch home was deeply carved in Arnold. It remained much more than a beautifully held memory. It influenced and encouraged and fired his ambition to achieve musical and cultural perfection and hence his whole life bore its effects. On every occasion he paid loving tribute.

In the Gabrilowitsch home his already growing love of chamber music was strengthened. This led to deeper study of it and greater participation. And step by step this led to the door that opened into conducting, and from there—but of that great phase of his life I shall tell later.

Professor Auer was a member of a magnificent quartet in which Karl Davidov played the 'cello. Davidov was not only a composer and great 'cellist (he had been solo 'cellist to the Czar since 1862) but an extraordinarily good teacher. For nine years he had been director of the Imperial Conservatory. When he resigned in 1887, Rubinstein came back as director.

That was the year Arnold entered.

Both Davidov and Auer were quick to recognize superior talents in the students and were equally noted for their benevolence toward those who were rich in ability but poor in money. Arnold was appointed official page turner for the quartet. He never missed a single concert. He attended most of the rehearsals, and his rapid development in playing that form of music confirms how much his attentive ear took in from this privileged association with these "noblemen of music."

In recalling those days, Arnold said, "I ate and drank chamber music. I lived it."

Auer, the marvelous coach, as well as great player, also had charge of the ensemble classes at the Conservatory. He indelibly influenced those who studied under him personally, and on down through the years his masterful methods and his superb spirit have been transmitted by them.

When Arnold studied under him, Auer was in the prime of life. He was only forty-five years old and already there lay behind him a long list of brilliant triumphs that gave firm foundation to his recognition as the greatest violin teacher. Yet this was long before the days he taught such later-distinguished virtuosos as Mischa Elman, Jascha Heifetz and many others.

Contemporary with Arnold, other Auer students of outstanding talent included Victor Walter, Boris Kamenski, Wolf Israel and Emil Milynarski. Arnold and Victor Walter, who was a little older, played a great deal of chamber music together. Victor became concertmaster of the Imperial Opera House Orchestra and later a music critic on a St. Petersburg paper.

Boris Kamenski, whose name Arnold rarely spoke without adding "he had a great talent" almost as if it were part of his name, was his roommate. Boris became leader of the orchestra organized by Prince Mechlenburg-Strelitsky.

Wolf Israel became a fine conductor and soloist and was

one of the first violinists of the Imperial Opera House.

Emil Milynarski went abroad to launch his notable career. He was a soloist, then symphony conductor, in Glasgow, Scotland, and returned to his native Warsaw as conductor of the opera and symphony orchestras. He composed very successfully, too. Later, his abilities became well known to Americans when, at Josef Hofmann's invitation, he came to conduct the Philadelphia Opera and the Curtis Institute Orchestra.

Auer made one of his wonder-children, Alexander Fidelman, change his name to Romanov. His destiny was especially dramatic for its surprising ups and downs—and fortunately an up again. After many years abroad he came to America in 1920, down and out. Arnold gave him an opportunity to appear as a soloist, after which he was engaged by the Los Angeles Philharmonic. It was but another proof of Arnold's ever-helping hand to musicians.

Auer's rank in music was based not only on his consummate power as a teacher, but as a superbly gifted virtuoso, and his powers extended into conducting with almost equal splendor. Besides being court violinist, he was founder, first violinist and musical director of the orchestra of the Imperial Russian Music Society. Luckily, there was a shortage of viola players, and Arnold had the distinction of being one of the students selected to play that instrument in the orchestra.

The concerts of the Imperial Russian Music Society were dazzling social events. The Czar attended every symphony, every opera and every ballet performance—with all his retinue. The huge figure of the autocratic Alexander III was always surrounded by a heavy military guard—great giants in full panoply. Hollywood with Technicolor and production budgets into the millions could not possibly portray the splendor—the brilliant uniforms, emblazoned with flashing decorations, worn so strikingly by the Czar, the cabinet and members of the royal family—the resplendent court dresses of the Czarina and her beautiful attendants. The grandeur beheld by the musicians from their side of the footlights was a far better sight than they afforded the audience.

Here was music elevated to the zenith of a nation's ability. No higher recognition could be achieved. The omnipotent of great Imperial Russia were here assembled to confirm the place of highest honor for music, to give inspiration to composers and performers, and by their applause to give homage to the surpassing powers of musical art. The Czar would usually confer his approval by inviting the conductor and the soloists to his box to thank them personally.

In Arnold's time, the guest conductors of the orchestra of the Imperial Russian Musical Society were Rimsky-Korsakov, Glazounov, Rubinstein, Safonoff, Liadov, Taniev, Vinogradski, Dvorak and Napraynik. Nikisch was imported from Leipzig. From Paris came Colonne and Lamoureux. Each gave one or two performances of his own compositions. The general opinion of the musicians of the orchestra was that string players made better conductors since they were better acquainted with the other instruments.

One of Arnold's honors while still a student was to play in a memorable quartet. It included Verghbilovitch, head of the 'cello department of the Conservatory, and Professor Nicolai Galkin, Arnold's teacher of violin during his first year. Both men drank heavily. It seemed, however, they played their best when under the influence. Once while the quartet was appearing at a prince's home, they nearly broke up the performance. They began fighting with their bows, but kept on playing in between. Alternately they used their bows for fencing foils and then for their proper purpose of producing music from their instruments, ceasing each lively exchange of wallops exactly on time to come in with their parts, then going at it again at the next rest. This ludicrous duel in the august atmosphere of the home of royalty so convulsed Arnold that it was he who, struggling to fight off laughter, could hardly continue playing.

"To Arnold Volpe in kind remembrance of December 3, 1890"—Tschaikowsky

"To Arnold Volpe in kind remembrance."—Anton Rubinstein

Arnold's talent was his easy entree into many of St. Petersburg's best homes. Besides, there was his buoyant personality, his delightfully lively eyes, and those always-glowing, ruddy cheeks. Exuberance and talent! Who could resist them?

Alexander Glazounov, whose home was in St. Petersburg, and Arnold were about the same age. They became fast friends. Glazounov had already composed his first symphony at the age of sixteen, and Arnold had the pleasure of playing many of his works while they were still in manuscript form. Arnold admired him extremely, not only for his almost unbelievable musical memory, but for his lovable personality.

The elder Glazounov was a well-known and wealthy publisher. He often entertained people of note in his home, and it was there Arnold met many of the great. Among other homes where he often played were those of General Cesar Cui and Prince Mechlenburg-Strelitsky. Both families were connected with the royal house.

Cesar Cui had just written his opera, *The Saracen,* and it was about to be heard for the first time in St. Petersburg. He himself was a colorful personality. The son of a French officer who couldn't follow Napoleon in his retreat from Moscow, he became an authority on fortifications after being graduated from the school of military engineering in St. Petersburg. In contrast to his interest in such huge constructions, he was also an effective painter of miniatures. Arnold was greatly fascinated by his many-sided intellect.

The favorite gathering place of all great musical celebrities was the home of the Davidovs. It was there Arnold met Rubinstein socially and Rimsky-Korsakov, Balakirev, Liadov and many other giants of the day.

What a rich memory of sympathetic and understanding association with artists who had already achieved imperishable recognition! What exciting camaraderie with other gifted students, who like Arnold were present to admire and adore.

I did not know much about all these experiences for many

years. They were so sacred to him that when he did talk of them there were usually tears in his eyes. His reverence for the great in music was deep and sincere. About his own accomplishments, he talked little; to him they were a gift of God for which he was humbly grateful.

The Davidov home was popular among the musically great, as much because of Davidov's personality as his high standing in music. He had been the director of the Conservatory. He had been especially praised for the greatly increased number of scholarships during his regime and for his personal efforts in finding free quarters for poor students. His ability as a 'cellist was without doubt extraordinary. But over and above all these, Arnold recalled, Davidov was a rare and perfect genius as a host. Soon after the sleighs with their jingling bells had deposited the guests on the steps of the Davidov home, the evening would begin with dinner. Then there were cards for some and music for others. It always ended with Rubinstein at the piano, playing for hours.

"Schumann was Rubinstein's favorite composer at that time," Arnold recalled. "Naturally, we always had the delight of listening to him play his own compositions."

To the students and faculty at the Conservatory, he would have been a revered personality — if only for his long and impressive connection with the institution. But Rubinstein had already grown to his immense stature in the musical world. Nearly thirty years before Arnold met him, Rubinstein had arrived in St. Petersburg to be court pianist and concert director, which position also carried a pension for life. He also conducted the concerts of the Imperial Music Society. He founded the Conservatory and was its first director. The Czar knighted him. Then for many years he was off on concert tours, including his American appearances in 1872-73. He had just returned from a series of "farewell" recitals throughout Europe and had taken up the reins of the Conservatory directorship again when Arnold received his scholarship.

At the keyboard Rubinstein was a wizard, not in the light modern sense of the word, but the literal, for the power he exerted over his audiences was truly magical. There were a few others, like Leopold Auer, who shared his authority in the musical realm, but very few. Arnold remembered sharply the impression Rubinstein made when, clapping his hands over his ears during a Wagner number, he rushed dramatically out of the concert hall. It was one of his milder ways of protesting that he was one hundred per cent anti-Wagner.

How greatly Rubinstein was acclaimed as a musician and as an immortal national figure was stamped in Arnold's memory by an exciting week of celebration held in November 1889 to honor Rubinstein's fifty years of musical activities. He had given his first concert at the age of six. The festivities included receptions by the Czar and by all civic societies, with each organization faced by the dual problem of being careful not to outshine the Czar's while at the same time attempting to surpass one another in their superlatives for Rubinstein. A banquet attended by the diplomatic representatives of all nations provided occasion for international eulogies. The week concluded with a large ball attended by all composers, and of course the students of the Conservatory Rubinstein had founded.

Chapter III
STUDENT MEMORIES

ONE OF ARNOLD'S most colorful memories of Anton Rubinstein included the Czar. Alexander III, accompanied always by his awesome military guard, would frequently visit the Conservatory on short notice. The Czar would send word in the morning and by noon be at the school. Rubinstein, meantime, would run nervously about getting the school alerted and as excited as he, for he usually managed to convey his tenseness to faculty and students.

The student orchestra would play for the Czar. Then he would inspect the great rooms and vast halls of the building and meet the faculty who, being experienced performers in the main, at least showed no outward sign of their inner dither. Finally, as the Czar and his party departed, to the diminuendo CLUMP-Clump-clump of the guard, the school breathed normally, and Rubinstein's aura of august composure again quickly encircled him—until the next imperial visit. It was but one of Arnold's many memories of the formal and serious atmosphere in which music was taught in the Conservatory.

Beginning with Arnold's second year, he received individual instructions from the great Auer, who always had other students present at the lessons. It has often occurred to me that this may have accounted in some measure for the excellence of his pupils later as teachers themselves. To watch and hear Auer teach, apparently, was to learn how to teach, as well as how to play. Professor Auer or Madame Stein, who later in the United States became Madame Auer, were always at the piano during lessons.

These were the years that were so important to Arnold Volpe's career. He did not talk much about them until many years later, when in retrospect he saw them in the full light of his own maturity. His confreres of those student days, who like himself later built splendid careers on the foundations laid at the Conservatory, also remembered with affection and fully understood their importance.

First, the faculty had been assembled from the ranks of the most brilliant and successful musicians in Europe. They were unsurpassed in their ability to teach. Since most of them were top-ranking performers or composers of repute and actual achievement, no student could accuse them of being only pedagogues and theorists. For example, Rubinstein's chief fame, indeed, was not as director of the Conservatory, nor Auer's as a violin *teacher,* and so on with the many others.

Students knew this. They came not only to learn from these masters, but to emulate. With good luck, they hoped possibly to equal them as performers, composers or conductors.

Moreover, students like Arnold Volpe were untroubled by any ferment of indecision as to why they were there or what they were going to do afterward. And for them the professors wholeheartedly poured out their knowledge, their skills, their affection and their intimate advice with the tender generosity of kindly adults who, having successfully climbed the ladder, reached down to help the next generation.

Although in the formal relationships of the faculty and students, the teachers maintained the positions of superiors, on one point there was complete equality. Even in those days, the Conservatory maintained a cafeteria, where for reasonable prices all could obtain their meals. The food available to students and teachers was the same.

I could never refrain from marveling at the wealth of exceptional advantages St. Petersburg provided for Arnold. Playing in quartets with such men as Galkin and Verghbilovitch and in the orchestra of the Imperial Russian Music Society never ceased to me to have been rich privileges for a youth. Just as important, and somehow more personally significant, were Arnold's associations with the incomparable

Gabrilowitsch family, with young Glazounov and his father, and all the assemblages of the mighty in music at the Davidov home, where Arnold and his gifted fellow students enjoyed ennobling friendships that would inspire them all their lives.

How often I heard Arnold and his old colleagues talk over those days, when they met in later years in New York, in Washington, in Kansas City, in Chicago and in Coral Gables.

Among all the experiences of his student days, there was a vivid one that took place when he was just past twenty. Peter Ilich Tschaikowsky — the great Tschaikowsky himself — was coming to the Imperial Conservatory of St. Petersburg to receive the homage of the institution from which he had been graduated. The occasion was Tschaikowsky's twenty-fifth anniversary as a composer.

The climax of the celebration was to be an evening of only Tschaikowsky's works. Arnold thought the high point had been reached when he was chosen to play the violin part in Tschaikowsky's well known *Piano Trio in A Minor,* which he had dedicated to Anton Rubinstein. Also, Arnold was to play the viola part in his string quartet. His gray eyes must have danced, his pink cheeks must have flushed even brighter with raptured excitement. But had he known what was to come....

The affair was a great success, musically and socially. The royal family was there, and so were the cream-of-the-cream of the musical world. After the concert Tschaikowsky expressed the wish to thank all the participants personally.

Arnold, when prodded into telling of the event, with characteristic modesty would begin by saying simply: "He was exceptionally kind to me in his praise for my part of the performance. I managed to ask him for a souvenir of the occasion —a photograph."

Then, as Arnold went on with the recollection, a lively light would come into his eyes, a new tone in his voice, touched with unsuppressed excitement, as he recounted: "Tschaikowsky said, 'Delighted! Come to my hotel tomorrow morning.' I was there at eight o'clock. Immediately I was admitted to his suite. He was still in his dressing gown and asked me to excuse his attire. He invited me to stay for breakfast. He kept me on until noon. I hung on every word. How can I describe in words those few hours! I was so filled with awe and gratitude for his cordiality and his fatherly interest in me. He advised me how and what to study, encouraging me to go on with my studies.

"He was so simple, so modest, so unassuming—the great Tschaikowsky spending an entire morning with a twenty-year-old student! The crescendo came when, fearing that I had already imposed upon his time, I arose to take leave and, honoring me after the Russian fashion, he kissed me.

"That was really more than I could stand, and I cried like a child. Tschaikowsky was moved by my sincerity and he, too, started to cry. For several minutes we stood embracing each other and weeping. It was the greatest moment of my life.

"After leaving the hotel, I walked the streets of St. Petersburg in a daze, living each second of that morning over and over again and repeating to myself, 'Tschaikowsky, the greatest living Russian composer, kissed me and encouraged me to go on with my studies.' "

Another deeply moving experience with Tschaikowsky took place later. Although it was several years later, Arnold always coupled the two events in his memory, and, indeed, they belong together. Arnold was present at the first performance of the *Pathetique Symphony,* held in the Salle de Noblesse. Tschaikowsky himself conducted. The musical elite and the royal family attended, and it was an immense event, both in the character of the audience and in its atmosphere of almost quivering anticipation.

"The ending of the last movement—slow, solemn, unexpected and unusual — brought forth much bewilderment," Arnold recalled. "There was an unmistakable lack of enthusiasm. No demonstration."

Even the opinion of the press and of the musicians was divided. Although some considered it his greatest work, most others differed. He had written it as his swan song and he was deeply disappointed. A week later Tschaikowsky was dead of cholera. Perhaps we shall never know whether the *Pathetique,* reflecting a morbid and fatalistic state of mind, foretold death by his own hand, or whether he drank that glass of unboiled water by accident. The circumstances attested by recent biographers would indicate the latter theory as probable. Herbert Einstock, in his book on Piotr Ilyitch, remarks that during the night of November 1, 1893, Tschaikowsky had suffered severe indigestion. In the morning, although unwell, he went out to pay some calls. He returned to luncheon with Modest and Bobyk. He poured out a tumbler of water, "brushed aside his companions' warnings that it was unboiled (cholera was epidemic in St. Petersburg at the time) and drank it off." His condition became progressively worse and the Drs. Bertenson were called. He recovered somewhat during the following day but soon relapsed into a coma and died during the afternoon of November 6.

Professors and selected honor students of the Conservatory were pallbearers. Arnold was one of the few students chosen. The walk beside the casket in that historic cortege forever engraved a gloomy mark in Arnold's memory.

Fortunately that gloom and grief were soon assuaged to some extent by another event that enlightened the musical world. The *Pathetique* Symphony was repeated in a memorial concert. The same orchestra played it. Napravnik conducted it with the same authentic interpretation. The same audience listened—but now with different ears. Tschaikowsky's swan song was now understood. The enthusiasm was beyond description. Of course, today it is one of the best known and most played symphonies of any composer.

Arnold's simply worded, frequent appraisal of Tschaikowsky was, "His music is an expression of his own great soul, combined with clever orchestral effects, highest technique and stirring melody."

Over the years, how frequently Arnold's conducting of Tschaikowsky's compositions revealed his full measure of admiration. How often as I heard him conduct the *Pathetique,* I knew his heart was crowded with memories of that morning in the hotel suite, the dull pain of the march beside the flower-draped casket, and the poignant ovation at the memorial concert.

Each performance he conducted of the *Pathetique* was for Arnold one more loving memorial to Tschaikowsky, to whose encouragement and interest in his career he owed so much.

Perhaps that in part explains Arnold's great love for all of Tschaikowsky's symphonies and other works, for at each performance, by striving for perfection, he aspired to make another worthy payment on that debt. I'm sure that is the way Tschaikowsky would accept it.

Chapter IV

CONSERVATORY HONORS

ALTHOUGH the Arnold Volpe collection of historical documents and letters covers only his own lifetime, some of these records tell of days that existed a very long time ago. It is not so much the dates they bear that make them so antiquated. It is the ideas they contain. The official Russian documents, particularly, seem almost unbelievably archaic to Americans.

When Arnold appeared for his final examination at the Conservatory in 1891 there was little difference from the academic procedures of our times. It was the wording of his diploma . . . but first let me tell of his examination.

He appeared before a board of professors. Anton Rubinstein presided as chairman. Arnold chose for his critical test to play the *Concerto* by Wieniawski and a Bach violin sonata. Ossip Gabrilowitsch, his beloved friend and fellow-student, played the piano accompaniment, an incident that always illuminated their lifetime of happy memories.

When Rubinstein spoke through music he was eloquent. It was equally well known that no matter how deep the feeling he was endeavoring to express, by comparison he was quite prosaic in his use of words. To those who understood this, however, he was never at a loss to convey either the strength of his opinions or the nuances of his emotions.

When Arnold finished playing, Rubinstein did not wait for the opinion of the committee. Although his words of congratulation themselves were simple—"This *is* violin playing!"—into his exclamation he put such fervor and enthusiasm that Arnold was justifiably recompensed for the many hardships he had endured during the four years at the Conservatory.

There was little in this method of examination that might

not take place in an institution of higher learning today. But let us read the text of Arnold's diploma:

"The Artists Society of the St. Petersburg Conservatory, Imperial Russian Musical Society, hereby decrees that the son of a privileged Kovno merchant, Arnold David Volpe, of Jewish origin, has studied at the St. Petersburg Conservatory in the violin classes of Professors Galkin and Auer and has been graduated in May, 1891, in the course of musical learning and is granted this diploma by the examining board with high standing.

"His chief talent was violin in the class of Professor Auer, where he qualified as first violin, and he was also outstanding in other subjects, the theory of music, piano-forte and the viola. He finished music, the theory of music and aesthetics and many learned musical subjects.

"Based on the foregoing high accomplishments and under laws 71 and 73 of the Conservatory of the Russian Imperial Musical Society and the Artists Society of the St. Petersburg Conservatory, the name of *Free Artist* and this diploma were deservedly granted to Arnold David Volpe on May 31, 1891. . . ."

Imagine an institution of higher learning in America issuing a diploma identifying the graduate by race, then in the same document granting legal exceptions and privileges to that individual!

The title "Free Artist" was as important to Arnold as was the recognition of his academic achievements.

The first music student to receive the title "Free Artist" from the St. Petersburg Conservatory was granted it in 1865. In those days Russia was anything but free, and the granting of this title opened up a new world to its recipients. From that time on musicians in Russia were really free to write what they would and how they would, to rise to positions of eminence in the artistic world and to travel wherever their talents dictated they must go.

After Arnold's first period at the Conservatory, he returned to Kovno to enter compulsory military service. Of the situation in Russia in those times, Arnold said later:

"The conditions under the Czar were very hard on the Jewish population. Only two per cent were allowed to enter schools of higher learning; education in general therefore was closed to most of them. The Jewish race as a whole is eager for learning, and these conditions naturally brought on rebellion and dissatisfaction. American youth has every reason to be grateful for having been born in this land of opportunity and freedom."

As one of those fortunate to be a graduate of an institution of higher musical learning, Arnold was permitted to "volunteer" for military service. "Volunteers" were required to serve only one year, instead of two. Also, instead of living in the barracks, they could live at home, so long as they appeared every day on the dot for drilling.

Arnold's music and his personal popularity had a further happy effect. The conductor of the orchestra at the Officers' Club recognized his talent and invited him to join the orchestra. Next, he turned the rehearsals over to Arnold. It was Arnold's first experience in conducting a full orchestra, and he loved it.

Because of his importance to the orchestra and a personal friendship that developed with the captain, Arnold appeared for drill, shall we say, irregularly.

"Rifle practice made me sick," he told me. "I was a bad marksman, very poor in drilling, and in fact so bad that when a high officer came to review us, he pointed me out as the poorest of all. The officers had to get me out of the jam. My interest was not in the gun, but in the bow—and not the kind with arrows, either."

When he took off his military uniform at the end of that bizarre year in Kovno and returned to St. Petersburg, it was so late in the season that all the better orchestras were filled.

In order to eat, he accepted a job as leader of one in a cheap resort on the outskirts. It was filled with playboys and women of bad repute, and to reach it at the opening hour he had to leave his room at four in the afternoon. Then, after playing until two a.m., he had a three-hour trip back—much too tired to appreciate the beauties of the summer dawn.

He suffered hardship and humiliation, for in his sensitive soul he felt such questionable surroundings were degrading to the art of music itself. He did not like the guilt of bringing it before the unappreciative habitues of such a place.

He was isolated, too, from all his old associates, and for the first time he realized that a musician's life is not entirely as sweet as it looks.

Later, at one of the beautiful summer resorts at Porlask, attended by fashionable and cultured people, Arnold played in an orchestra conducted by Professor Galkin. He commissioned Arnold to compose something for him. It was a waltz, *Souvenir de Porlask,* and it received an ovation. But I never heard it played, for Arnold later destroyed it along with many others which in his stern perfectionism he considered immature.

In 1893, Arnold re-entered the Imperial Conservatory, on the advice of Rubinstein, who told him that he had the ability to go much further. His interest was in composition, ensemble music and conducting. His destiny was decided when Rubinstein added to his astute advice and warm encouragement by granting him another four-year scholarship. Besides the joy of renewing old friendships, he had the satisfaction of a good position with the theatre orchestra as concertmaster.

Although he supported himself by playing, he "neglected" his violin. He threw himself ardently into music theory, composition and counterpoint, with what results we need only look at later achievements to discover.

From the beginning, even as a child, he was interested in the music of many instruments. Now, in ensemble work he was in his element. What an inspiration, could he have foreseen future recognition. But he scarcely needed these future kudos then. His own zeal sufficed.

He had the choice of entering the classes of Nikolai Soloviev or Rimsky-Korsakov. Their contemporaries considered them both outstanding. Soloviev was a little older. Arnold chose his classes. He had, however, the benefit of the criticism and guidance of Rimsky-Korsakov, for the latter headed the examination board. Rimsky-Korsakov always gave Arnold the highest marks, and his written exercises were used as examples.

Arnold's fugues and inventions were later introduced to the higher classes. It was very pleasant to bask in the prestige this gave him among the students, as well as among the faculty. I have used a word here to denote his feeling of satisfaction. But "bask" is actually far from the right word. He took time for nothing so leisurely, either figuratively or literally. It was not that in his busy, ebullient youth he did not enjoy himself, but his pleasures came mainly from plunging into his studies.

"I fully realized," he told me years later, "that in order to become a good conductor, it was not enough to play an instrument well, but equally essential to acquire knowledge in all fields of music—to learn to analyze scores of all schools, a skill that can be mastered only by an intense study of music history, composition and every branch connected with them."

One of his great inspirations was Alexander Glazounov, who predicted a fine career for Arnold as a writer of music. He said to him, "Volpe, you have the making of a great composer. Remember, however, it might mean starvation." Later, let me tell you what Glazounov said at a happy meeting thirty years after, in New York.

As a composer Arnold received his second diploma from the Imperial Conservatory in 1897, bearing the special statement, "With high standing and marked success," and the further praise, "outstanding in canon and fugues."

Most of Arnold's compositions were begun during his student days and later revised. For instance, his *Quartet in A Major* was originally a piano sonata. It has been played by many well-known quartets. Of his violin pieces, the *Mazurka* is best known. His songs met with success.

In speaking of his music years later, he said: "My compositions are far from modern. I find the modern music most interesting, but it is not in my blood as is the music of the older Russia and the classics."

But in the years to come, conducting was to be his chief work. When others asked why he had not composed more he replied: "I was never able to divide my time between two such important musical activities; one took everything I had to give."

Meanwhile, he had also received by Imperial decree the privileges of "Honorable Citizen of Russia" or, as it is sometimes translated, "Personally Honored Citizen." This gave him the distinction of possessing the *right to reside anywhere* in Russia.

He had come knocking timidly on Professor Auer's door only a few years before. Now, his talent and his gumption and his energy had earned him freedom.

When he explained this to me, he added crisply:

"Believe me, I am much prouder of my American citizenship papers."

After being graduated from the Imperial Conservatory, he was offered an important position there if he would become converted to the Christian faith. Arnold explained this to me: "I had no affiliations with any church then, and it would have made no difference one way or the other to me. But my love for my mother kept me from hurting her."

Also, there was his keen desire to see something of the world outside of St. Petersburg. One can imagine the hunger for new horizons in a young man of thirty who had spent most of his life in intense musical study.

He recalled the glowing remarks about America that Tschaikowsky had made at the Rubinstein celebration.

But Arnold's father, still the stern dissenter, had taken a violent dislike to the young man for whom Arnold's only sister had formed an attachment. To break it off, he had taken her to South Africa. There they had been joined by Arnold's mother and two of Arnold's brothers. So Arnold, taking his three younger brothers, journeyed to Johannesburg in 1897 to visit the family.

He gave several successful concerts and organized the Johannesburg Philharmonic Orchestra, with resulting approbation from the elite of the city and such acclaim from newspaper critics as "a musician of first rank," "exceptionally well done," and "he captivated his audience."

But the field was limited. He had decided to return to Russia when he became infatuated with a Canadian pianist he met in Capetown. She was leaving for London, and Arnold and a friend, a fine 'cellist, made the same boat. Perhaps, like Arnold, I may pass lightly over this romance.

Arnold and his 'cellist friend were travelling steerage, for they were broke. Their good clothes, however, belied the condition of their pockets and enabled them to break the ship's rules and mingle above decks with the first-class passengers, among whom Arnold promptly found another attractive pianist, Ella Russell.

She in turn discovered, not only Arnold's excellent musical ability and his bad financial condition, but that he was extremely attractive. This led her to solve all facets of the problem. She arranged a concert on the ship and accompanied Arnold in a group of solos which so delighted the passengers that the receipts, in the form of a purse of gold, constituted what he always referred to as "a fortune."

When the ship reached England six weeks later, Arnold was able to entertain Miss Russell in style as the romance blossomed. Under its inspiration he earnestly studied English. But

Rimsky-Korsakov

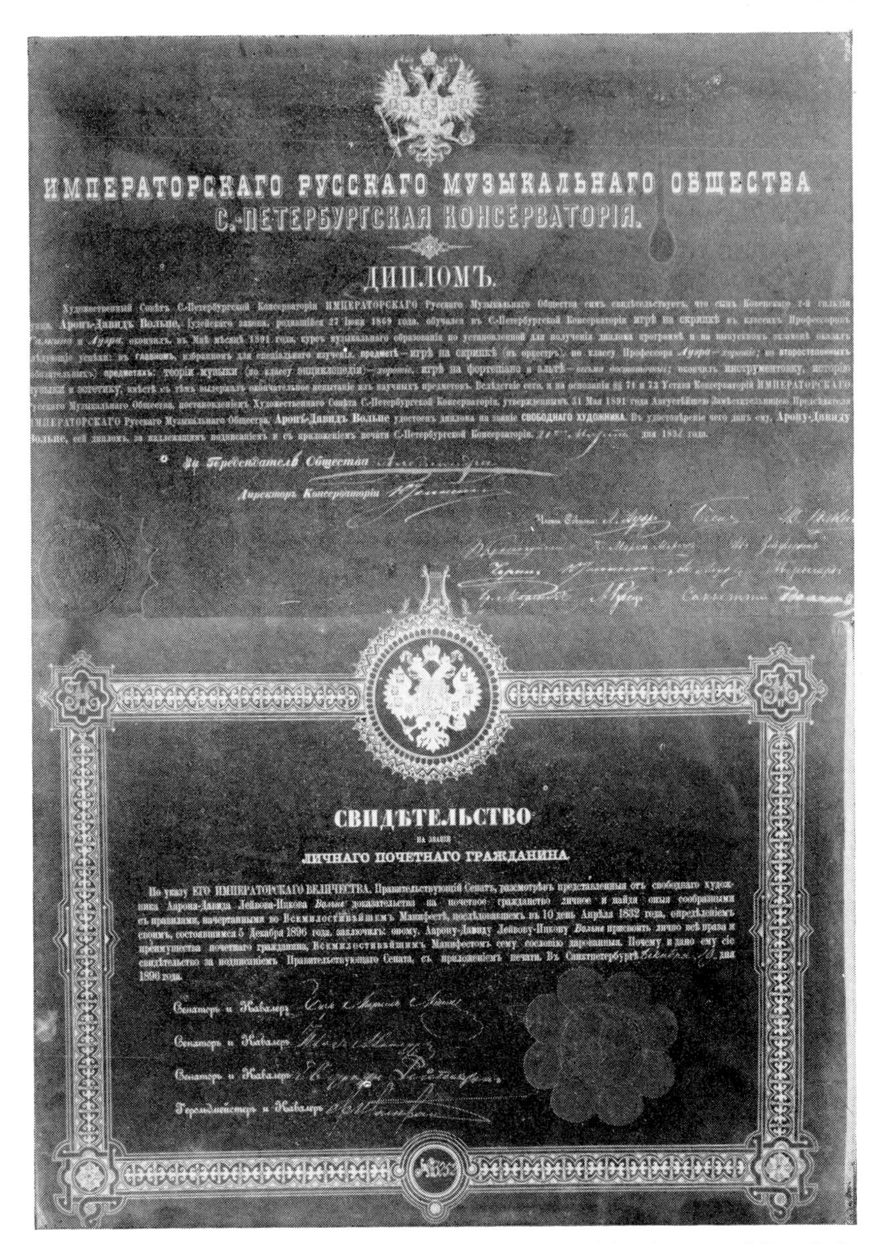

ИМПЕРАТОРСКАГО РУССКАГО МУЗЫКАЛЬНАГО ОБЩЕСТВА
С.-ПЕТЕРБУРГСКАЯ КОНСЕРВАТОРІЯ.

ДИПЛОМЪ.

За Предсѣдателя Общества

Директоръ Консерваторіи

СВИДѢТЕЛЬСТВО
на званіе
ЛИЧНАГО ПОЧЕТНАГО ГРАЖДАНИНА

Сенаторъ и Кавалеръ

Сенаторъ и Кавалеръ

Сенаторъ и Кавалеръ

Герольдмейстеръ и Кавалеръ

Top: "Granted on May 31, 1891 deservedly to Arnold David Volpe the name of Free Artist and this diploma was given to Arnold David Volpe with the seal and the signature of the St Petersburg Conservatory on March 21, 1892."

Certificate to honor Personally Honored Citizen "By decree of His Imperial Highness and the authorized Senate, after perusal of the documents pertaining to Student Arnold Volpe . . ."—Dec. 19, 1896 this new facility in the language was soon turned to another purpose.

A former schoolmate, George Russato, turned up in London on his way to America. George was a cultured youth, a graduate doctor of medicine. But he loved music above all else and had given up a good practice to become a tenor. His family, should we say, did not understand him.

He was broke and could get no further than London. Arnold paid for his passage, and together, with rosy visions of what lay before them, they sailed for America.

Arnold planned only a visit. He sincerely intended to return to Russia.

Chapter V

NEW YORK—1899-1904

ARNOLD VOLPE enjoyed the close companionship of other people.

During the years before he sailed for New York he had been among warm, musically minded friends. In the lively musical fellowship of St. Petersburg, he had been a beloved and popular figure.

But New York was different. He was unknown; at least he felt unknown. New York, like the rest of the United States early in the century, was filled with excitement over the Spanish-American War, just concluded. He could not help being affected to some extent by all this patriotic ardor. He was impressed, but more interested in New York's musical condition, which to him seemed sad.

As he looked about for a job, George Russato, who shared a room with him, committed suicide. Although the musical condition of New York had nothing to do with George's despondency (lack of sympathy from his family drove him to this strait), the untimely death of his friend lent a gloomy cast to Arnold's first months in America. He missed his roommate, all his old friends in St. Petersburg, and his daily association with the great men of Russian music.

Especially did he miss the all-pervading atmosphere of musical idealism. He couldn't find it then in New York, and he was still very much under the spell of his rich memories and the prestige of the Imperial Conservatory.

So on his first job, at Shanley's, then a fashionable restaurant, Arnold disguised his identity behind dark glasses. Later he criticized this youthful act as false pride.

Soon he was playing in the few orchestras then existing in New York—The People's Symphony, under F. X. Ahrens, the

Symphony Society under Walter Damrosch and the Hermann Hans Wetzler Orchestra, with which Richard Strauss made his first American appearance as conductor at John Wanamaker's, 10th Street and Broadway.

Wetzler, a musical millionaire, had organized the orchestra in 1903 and was instrumental in bringing Strauss, even then dubbed "Richard the Lesser" and hailed as a "magnificent rebel" among composers, to his first American venture. Strauss conducted his first pair of concerts with the Wetzler ensemble, on April 8 and 16, 1904, and Arnold was a part, albeit a very small part, of this historic occasion.

EDUCATIONAL ALLIANCE
NEW YORK
Series of 6 HISTORICAL
CONCERTS of
CHAMBER MUSIC

Sixth and Last Concert
SATURDAY, MAY 13TH, 1899,
AT 8:15 P. M.
E. Bernstein . . . . *Pianist*
A. Volpe . . . . *Violinist*
M. Altschuler . . *Violoncellist*

Programme

PART I

TRIO. In D minor for Piano, Violin and Cello *A. Arensky*
Messrs. E. Bernstein, A. Volpe and M. Altschuler

PART II

SONATA. In D major, for Piano and Cello *A. Rubinstein*
Messrs. E. Bernstein and M. Altschuler

PART III

TRIO. In A minor, for Piano, Violin and Cello *P. Tschaikowsky*
Messrs. E. Bernstein, A. Volpe and M. Altschuler

By then, some of his former schoolmates had learned of his arrival. Among them were the Altschuler brothers with whom he had been closely associated in their Warsaw student days. How the New York audiences who soon saw them together would have laughed had they been able to visualize Arnold and Modest Altschuler as they lived in Warsaw. But the audiences saw them only as accomplished and serious young artists allied in a trio with an equally talented pianist, Eugene Bernstein. They played many a concert together at the Educational Alliance, Cooper Union, and elsewhere for the next several years.

As Arnold continued to establish himself as a player of chamber music, he composed and, at the same time, laid the foundations for his long career as a teacher of the violin. From the start, his classes grew steadily. Many gifted boys were among his students, most of them too poor to pay for their lessons. This did not help financially, but it gave Arnold another welcomed chance to repay the opportunities extended to him. Among the students who benefited from his payment to the past were Louis Edlin, Max Barr, Harry Weisbach and Samuel Lifshey. All made splendid careers.

On March 6, 1900, when the world, and especially New York, was still very much awhirl over the turn of the century, a program of Arnold's compositions was presented with great success by a group of representative music patrons at the Carnegie Lyceum, connected with Carnegie Hall. The concert included some of his chamber music, a number of his piano works played by Eugene Bernstein, and a group of songs sung by Mrs. Morris Black, contralto. The critics were enthusiastic.

Recognition was coming to Arnold in many ways.

The Altschuler brothers invited him to join them in a quartet sponsored by Edward J. de Coppet, the great patron of chamber music. Mr. de Coppet, in Arnold's oft-expressed opinion, did as much for chamber music in New York as Major Henry Lee Higginson did for the symphony by founding and supporting so freely the Boston Symphony Orchestra.

Mr. de Coppet, an American banker of Swiss descent, engaged the quartet by the year. At the de Coppet home, 314 West Eighty-fifth Street, it performed every Sunday afternoon before distinguished audiences, not of the "Who's who of music in America" then, but of the "Who's who of the Who's who."

Here was art—performed with minute attention to perfection—in an atmosphere of cloistered adoration. Arnold was engrossed in these concerts.

Engrossed is indeed the right word to describe Arnold's bachelor years in New York. He was not only deep in music, but in the study of languages. Besides his native Russian, which I always considered so difficult that even a Russian must have to labor with it, he mastered German, French, Polish and English. Later he took up Italian and Spanish.

Meanwhile, he had brought his mother and father and two younger brothers to New York and set them up in a comfortable home. Nevertheless, he was still dreaming of some day going back to Russia, with understandable visions of triumphs in the old rosily remembered atmosphere of St. Petersburg, and he still retained his Russian citizenship. Obviously he had no time nor thoughts for young ladies.

As a Russian subject, he had to report every three years for three weeks of military service. In the summer of 1901, just the day before he was to sail for this duty, we first met.

Arnold and I were born in the same city of Kovno. Our parents knew each other there, but mine had taken me at the age of two to Berlin, where I lived until we came to New York. My parents were prosperously engaged in the wholesale processing and selling of ostrich feathers, in those days quite a large industry. The beautiful plumes were gathered as a crop, so to speak, from domesticated birds on ranches in South Africa and California.

Mother was known among the executives and workers as "The mother of the ostrich feather trade," a title she bore appropriately because of her excellent business ability. She was a beautiful and brilliant woman, but at home a tyrant. My father was a kindly soul, a serious Hebrew scholar, descended from a long rabbinical line, who knew nothing of business and cared nothing about it.

Mother, whom I assisted in the business, and I usually went home together, travelling on the Madison Avenue streetcar. With us on that memorable day was Joseph Mandelkern, a friend of the family and well-known in musical circles, who had been responsible for bringing some of the greatest Russian dancers to this country. When we reached 70th Street, an attractive young man boarded the car. He immediately greeted Mr. Mandelkern who, in turn, introduced him to us as Arnold Volpe. Mother and I left the car at 86th Street where we lived. Arnold sailed for Russia the following day.

He claimed that during his absence I was never for a moment out of his thoughts, and when he returned to New York, he asked Mother's permission to call. She urged me to wear a certain pretty dress to look my best. I just laughed and wore a simple skirt and blouse and all evening behaved like a filly. I was young, full of girlish fun, and not interested in marriage or musicians.

I was, however, interested in music, having studied voice since I was sixteen. My sister Henriette was a pianist, even then with professional ambitions. Across the street lived Albert von Doenhoff and Arthur Loesser, also pianists. In order to determine the championship between their household and ours, as to who could play the loudest, they and Henriette would sometimes open the windows and hammer away. It was a contest in which I cheered neither side, for my sympathies were with the neighbors of 86th Street.

Arnold's appearance upon our household scene gave rise to a contest of quite another sort. I was already being courted by a young man of promise in the millinery business, and evening after evening they would arrive at the same time. As the clock began to indicate that it would soon be time for them to leave, they would eye each other, both hoping the other would leave first. Their looks became glares, one trying to eliminate the other by sheer ocular warfare. Finally, as this did not work, and the clock at last required their departure, they would stalk out together. I never learned what they said to each other outside.

Both proposed the same day. Neither was accepted. I was not interested in being married. But Arnold was not easily discouraged, and I had my first demonstration of his will-power.

My mother recognized his sterling qualities. She was even more disgusted with me than were my two sisters and my brother. On one of Arnold's visits, she asked him to hear me sing. He was enthusiastic about my voice and offered to help me become a singer. But I did not crave a career. Then he tried to win me with his violin. I naturally recognized his artistry. And that was all.

Early in the autumn, however, I asked him to come to hear me sing for the high holidays, and to attend services and fast in the large temple. Not only was he uninterested in religion, he had never been in a church except to learn the ecclesiastical forms of music. Anything, however, to enhance his chances to win me! He came and he fasted.

Later in the fall, his mother became seriously ill. When the doctor gave up hope for recovery, Arnold beseeched me to meet his mother before she died. He knew, he told me afterward, that I would have to yield after I met her. She was so desperately ill, but so gracious and sweet to me. Holding my hands, she kept asking questions. Her only thought was for her eldest and favorite son whose love and devotion and anguish at losing her were pathetic, beautiful and sincere. I was beginning to weaken.

We became engaged on November 10, 1901. His mother passed away on November 28. We were married April 15th, 1902, in the large temple at Seventy-second Street and Lexington Avenue where I had been singing. Arnold's dear friend, Eugene Bernstein, was his best man.

First Letters

160 East 70th Street
August 6, 1901

My dear Miss Michelson,

It was my intention to call on you very soon after the evening of our meeting. Unfortunately, it was impossible for me to do so, owing to my mother's sickness.

I am quite in despair since the doctors have declared her disease serious.

May I ask you to let me know if it will be convenient for you to receive me Saturday evening or Sunday.

Hoping to see you soon, and with kind regards to Mr. and Mrs. Michelson and your sisters.

Yours very sincerely,
Arnold Volpe

160 East 70th Str.
August 6th 1901.

My dear Miss Michelson.

It was my inten[tion]
to call on you very soo[n]
after the evening of o[ur]
meeting. Unfortunat[ely]
it was impossible for [me]
to do so, owing to [my]
mother's sickness.

I am quite i[n]

since [illegible]
has [illegible]
M[illegible]
know[illegible]
for you[illegible]
evening on Sunday.

Hoping to see you [illegible]
and with kind re[gards]
to Mr & Mrs Mich[elson]
and your sister

Yours very sincerely
Arnold Volpe

66 East 86 Str.
September 6 '01.

Dear Mr Volpe

I have
received your kind letter
and was more than sorry
to hear about your dear
mother's illness. My family
as well as myself sincerely
wish her a speedy recovery.
I shall be very pleased
to have the pleasure of
your company on next
Sunday evening, as we may
come back till family
business on Saturday.

With kindest regards
from my dear parents and
sisters

Sincerely yours
[illegible] Michelson

First Letters.

66 East 86th Street
September 6, 1901

Dear Mr. Volpe,

I have received your kind letter and was more than sorry to hear about your dear mother's illness. My family, as well as myself, sincerely wish her a speedy recovery.

I shall be very pleased to have the pleasure of your company in our house Sunday evening, as we may come home late from business on Saturday.

With kindest regards from my dear parents and sisters.

Sincerely yours,
Marie Michelson

Arnold was nearly thirty-three years old. I was but twenty. His intimate associates and friends had warned him he was marrying too young a woman. His answer was, "Oh well, I can always go back to my first love, my violin."

It was the only rival of whom I ever had reason to be jealous; no man ever expressed or lived greater love and devotion to a woman. He was a one-woman man throughout his life.

Many years after our marriage, his devoted children asked him to put down some of his impressions of that time. I quote verbatim what he wrote:

"I boarded the street car at Seventieth Street, and on it I met a friend, Joseph Mandelkern, a familiar figure in the musical world. With him were two ladies, Mrs. Michelson and her daughter Marie.

"As soon as I was introduced, I knew the daughter was the woman for me. She was young, full of charm and beauty, yet so unconscious of it all.

"During my entire trip abroad, I could not get her out of my mind. On my arrival in Russia, when friends asked why I had not married, I would reply: 'I have met her!'

"Immediately on my return to New York, I began calling. I must admit that I did not win Marie Michelson as easily or as quickly as I had hoped. But I would have gone on courting her the rest of my life. There was no other woman for me. No man ever found greater happiness or devotion."

I was immediately welcomed by his large and distinguished circle of friends and colleagues. And from Europe came a letter from his friend since youthful days, Pauline Gabrilowitsch:

St. Petersburg,
19 April, 1902

Dear Arkádee Lvovitch:

First of all allow me to congratulate you from my soul on your engagement and wish you most heartily all of the best and much happiness! Your letter gave me much joy. I was already thinking that you forgot about our existence. But now I know the reason of your long silence. I can imagine what you and yours experienced during all this time. . . . It is not always easy to live in this world. But rather we find in everybody's life difficult moments which are not easy to overcome! . . . But now I think you are happy and can look forward courageously. Tell me, how is your bride? An American, a Russian or a Jewish girl? . . . Have you known her a long time? See, I predicted that you will soon find a person that is worthy of you—Now my words came true.

And how are your musical affairs? How is your quartet? Any more teaching? Ossip is now in Paris. I wrote him about your engagement. Say, why have you suddenly begun to write me in English? Do you think I do not understand Russian well? Or are you hesitating in writing Russian? Why? It can only be useful for you—otherwise you will forget the Russian language altogether. Even if you make a mistake nobody will object. But please you just write in any language you wish, but write. From me you will of course not get any English language letters.

In Petersburg the season is rather lively—Nikisch and Muller are here to direct concerts. Also played Thibaud, a violinist from Paris, Pechnikov and others. There are many theatrical troupes. German, French and the Italian Opera. Do you remember Kamenski? He was in NYC and had a great success. Now that we received your letter we are all most happy to congratulate you and to wish you all of the best. We know your character and are sure that you made an excellent choice. We are therefore certain that you will be satisfied with one another and will be very happy. All our friends join in sending you most cordial congratulations.

Yours,
Pauline Gabrilowitsch

My life changed abruptly from the surroundings of business

to art. My recollections of the Sunday afternoons of chamber music at the de Coppets' are especially treasured. They helped quickly to dispel my misgivings as to whether I would like a life so largely concentrated on music and musicians.

I can still see Mr. de Coppet, in the front row, with his earphone, listening to the concert. He had a discerning taste and a highly cultivated understanding. Mrs. de Coppet was a splendid pianist and often played piano with the quartet.

314 WEST 85TH STREET

Programme
March 28th, 1901

BEETHOVEN
Quartet—Op. 59—in E minor
MESSRS. KARGER, VOLPE,
J. & M. ALTSCHULER

ARNOLD VOLPE
Andante sostenuto; Allegro moderato.

AUGUST MEYER
Poco adagio & Molto cantabile.

NAPRAVNIK
Scherzo—Russian danse.
MESSRS. KARGER, VOLPE,
J. & M. ALTSCHULER

SCHUMANN Piano Trio—No. 3—Op. 110—in G minor
(a) Bewegt, doch zu rasch.
(b) Ziemlich langsam.
(c) Rasch.
(d) Kraftig, mit Humor.
MRS. DE COPPET,
MESSRS. VOLPE & ALTSCHULER.

All members of the quartet had a contract with Mr. de Coppet. It stipulated a definite number of hours for the daily rehearsal. The two Altschuler brothers, who were in charge of the personnel, called rehearsals any time that suited *them*. Often this would be midnight, after they had finished playing an engagement. They were rather Bohemian, and except for appearances at performances, nothing so regular as a clock controlled their lives.

As long as Arnold was a bachelor, it didn't matter much to him when the Altschulers' mood for rehearsing might seize them. But after we were married, he asked them to arrange regular rehearsal hours, either day or evening as they pleased, but regular. This brought resentment from the Altschulers.

They went to Mr. de Coppet, saying that Arnold *refused* to rehearse. Since Modest and Jacob were in charge, and Mr. de Coppet naturally heard nothing from Arnold, the decision was left up to the Altschulers. Arnold was replaced.

Early one Sunday morning—less than two months later—I answered the doorbell. It was Mr. de Coppet himself to tell Arnold he had just heard the truth and had taken action.

314 West 85th street

Programme

December 21st, 1902

Mozart
Quartet
(a) Allegro
(b) Larghetto
(c) Menuetto; moderato
(d) Allegro assai.
MESSRS. POCHON, SPARGUR, VOLPE, & EBANN.

Paul Juon
Sonata for Piano and Viola, Op. 15, in D.
(a) Moderato
(b) Adagio assai e molto cantabile; poco piu mosso.
(c) Allegro moderato.
MRS. DE COPPET & MR. POCHON

Anton Dvorak
Quartet, Op. 106, in G.
(a) Allegro moderato.
(b) Adagio ma non troppo
(c) Molto vivace
(d) Andante sostenuto; allegro con fuoco.
MESSRS. POCHON, SPARGUR, VOLPE, & EBANN.

Although Arnold had looked on the Altschulers' prevarication more or less as a prank, Mr. de Coppet had not. They were no longer with the quartet, Mr. de Coppet said. Would Arnold come back and take charge? He did. Nevertheless, in a spirit of give and take which somehow infuses most musicians, Arnold and the Altschulers always remained friends.

The first year of married life took quite a bit of adjusting, for Arnold had some strange bachelor habits. His mind was so often not on the routines of life. On a streetcar or bus, he would dreamily pay his own fare—and forget mine. At our destination, he would arise automatically, jump off and hurry away, completely oblivious that I was there, struggling to catch up—until I called, "Wait a minute; remember, you have a wife now."

It was all done so innocently out of unconscious habit that no one could take offense, and it always ended in a big laugh.

How gay and clear such little things come back to me over the years.

He had another habit, which I then thought was really bad. He drank hot tea all day long it seemed—two glasses for breakfast; more again at ten o'clock in the morning, served in his studio; more again at four; more for dinner; and more before retiring. I feared it would undermine his health.

But he was always robust—and he looked it. His sparkling gray eyes and his clear skin, with his cheeks always cheerfully, bloomingly pink, and his springy step—all belied my fears about tea.

Perhaps he inherited his physical vigor. At any rate, he

maintained it through his love of walking. I remember particularly his early morning studies of Italian just after we were married. Every day, before going into the studio, he would pick up his Italian book, stride off to Central Park, and walk round and round the reservoir, book in hand, for at least an hour, exercising both his keen facility for languages and his muscular legs.

Arnold was always well dressed. He used to say, "One of my weaknesses, even as a student, was to be a good dresser. A great deal of my earnings was spent on clothes, and later my good wife indulged me still more. All my clothes had to be custom tailored. My respect to the man who made most of them! Samuel Grossman was an artist in his line."

Mr. Grossman's son Benjamin became one of Arnold's violin pupils. A good amateur violinist and firm admirer of Arnold, he expressed his appreciation of his teacher by being responsible for publishing Arnold's *Quartet*.

Chapter VI

YOUNG MEN'S SYMPHONY ORCHESTRA—1902-1919

I HAVE already spoken of Arnold's large violin classes.

They not only grew and grew from the very first, but they attracted so many students whose talents were especially outstanding. Musically ambitious young men, and some women, recognized the opportunity to benefit by his thorough and exceptional training.

At the same time, Arnold felt deeply that by passing on his rich knowledge to the younger generation, he could, in a sense, repay what he had received from Professors Auer and Galkin and all the rest in St. Petersburg.

As his students advanced in ability, it was not long before they asked a very pointed question: "What next?" Yes, what indeed was there for them to do after they had mastered their instruments?

There was no opportunity in the America of 1902 for graduate instrumental students to learn orchestral routine. It is different nowadays. Many student and amateur orchestras—like the National Orchestral Association, designed to remedy just such a paucity of opportunity; the High School of Music and Art and the Juilliard School of Music in New York; the Curtis Institute in Philadelphia; the Peabody Conservatory in Baltimore and other large conservatories throughout the country—now afford this outlet. There was nothing of the kind in 1902.

Americans are wont to think back over a miraculous history of advancement. We remember our increase in population, our fabulous inventions, industrial growth and magnificent strides.

But how often do we consider our tremendous progress in music? How frequently do we think of the orchestral pioneers, who have labored since the turn of the century?

It never occurred to Arnold Volpe, the young student in St. Petersburg, to wonder how the orchestra of the Imperial Conservatory came into being. It was so obviously a necessity in rounding out a musical education. Unconsciously, he knew this. He knew, too, of course, that musical education had been going on in Russia for a very long time.

In the United States it had only a brief and scanty history. He knew this, too. But when he was actually faced with the facts in New York, he could not help being shocked. There were no orchestras for the training of young musicians.

America was not producing its own orchestral artists. It imported them from abroad. If one had asked, "Why not use domestic products?" the answer would have been, "Why bother? The imported ones come fully trained and fully experienced."

When Arnold appraised this situation, he changed fully from Volpe the Russian to Volpe the American.

While Arnold was considering how to fill this need of young students, Mr. de Coppet decided to form the Flonzaley Quartet, so named for his summer estate near Lake Geneva, Switzerland. Before Mr. de Coppet left for Europe to launch this organization for public performances, Arnold was invited to join it. What a temptation! How Arnold loved chamber music! It would be a delightful life and a well paid one. He was an admirer of Mr. de Coppet and all the quartet members, and they were warm friends.

I have before me now, as I write, a time-stained postcard bearing a message from Vienna. It reveals Arnold's answer to the invitation to become a member of the Flonzaley Quartet. Dated Nov. 22, 1903, it says:

"At the annual St. Cecilia dinner, the undersigned drink the health of their New York musical friends."

It was signed by E. J. de Coppet, Pauline de Coppet, and all four members of the Flonzaley Quartet. Arnold had chosen to remain in New York. He had felt the stronger challenge of America's need for a student training orchestra, and went after it with characteristic force and sincerity.

As the idea of the student orchestra kept growing in his thoughts, he talked it over with his students. They became enthusiastic, begging him to bring the idea into realization. It seemed to answer the questions constantly uppermost in their minds: What is there for us to do after we master our instruments? Where do we go next?

Arnold did not have the means to start such a movement himself. It would take money for music, stands, and a place to rehearse. His friends in the musical world were increasing. He was playing a great deal of chamber music with different groups. In one of them was Alfred Lincoln Seligman, a patron of music and a good amateur 'cellist.

One day Arnold told my sister Henriette, then a protégée of the Seligman family, about his idea. Although she was still in her teens, she immediately recognized the great value of such an institution to the coming musicians, and she told Mr. Seligman about it.

Mr. Seligman was a colorful and active personage in the world of arts. Soon after he was graduated from Columbia University in 1882, he had gone West. He gave up the post of treasurer of the Anglo-California Bank, to devote himself to painting and music. He was the youngest brother of Isaac N. Seligman of J. and W. Seligman and Co., bankers.

Arnold always remembered how he had stood, cold and alone and frightened, on the steps of the Imperial Conservatory, hungering for a chance to become a fine musician. So, on behalf of the young musicians of New York, who hungered for musical education, and—as it turned out later—on behalf of thousands of others in the years to come, Arnold again stood on the steps.

Eugene Bernstein and Arnold Volpe

Arnold Volpe and Alfred Seligman

Young Men's Symphony Orchestra, 1903

Young Men's Symphony Orchestra, 1915

This time when he tipped his hat, it was only figuratively. Instead of asking of Professor Auer, "Have you heard?" he said to Alfred Seligman, "Let me tell." He was no longer the poor unknown boy on the steps of the Conservatory. He was the well-known teacher and recognized musician. He was "steamed up," too, by the knowledge that he was speaking on behalf of deserving young Americans.

Mr. Seligman listened carefully. He agreed to back the orchestra. As an amateur musician of ability, he knew how much orchestral training was needed by the individual, a fact he attested by reserving for himself the right always to hold the first chair in the 'cello section. Faithfully, he attended every rehearsal.

After the first few years, however, he did not agree with Arnold on all points. He did not think it important for the orchestra to give concerts, while Arnold, as a professional musician, was fully aware of the psychological necessity of public appearances, knowing the immense effect on musicians of looking forward to performances before audiences and critics. Arnold considered it an essential part of the training. Nevertheless, because of Mr. Seligman's views, very few concerts were given in the early years.

This historic venture was to be called "The Young Men's Symphony Orchestra of New York." Its initials—YMSO—had a powerful and delightful significance in the field of American music for many years. Arnold conducted it from 1902 through 1919. It is difficult now to estimate the total influence it had on the development of orchestral music in this country.

Let me quote from the first printed folder announcing it. This modestly worded document is not precisely a "Bill of Rights," but in describing a new opportunity for musicians bearing the "Trained in America" label, it had a meaning very much akin to it. The pamphlet said:

> Its object is to promote orchestral efficiency, routine and experience among prospective professional musicians, so that they

may be sooner and better equipped to take their places in the musical life and orchestras of the city.

This Society therefore aims to provide the same opportunity for the rising generations of musicians which, in Europe, the students enjoy in the endorsed conservatories and music schools, namely, ensemble playing of the best orchestral music within their musical and technical scope.

This movement is an educational one, and by assisting it the music-loving public will benefit in proportion to the orchestral efficiency acquired by the young men through this Society.

The establishment of chamber music classes, work in harmony, lectures on musical subjects by competent authorities, and free musical tuition to those unable to pay are among the prospective plans. A concert will be given at the close of the season to which all subscribers and friends are cordially invited.

Rehearsal meetings are held weekly under the conductorship of Arnold Volpe, at the Mendelssohn Glee Club Hall, No. 108 West 55th Street, Sunday mornings at 10:30.

Nominal dues of 25¢ per month have been established, as well as a penalty for tardiness or absence unless unavoidable and notice has previously been given.

Applications for membership may be obtained from the Secretary of the organization at the rehearsals, as above indicated.

The following had signed this manifesto as directors: F. X. Ahrens, Dr. I. L. Hill, F. Von Inten, A. L. Seligman and Arnold Volpe.

After the first year there was always a long waiting list of applicants for membership. For seventeen years Arnold conducted the Young Men's Symphony Orchestra, without missing one rehearsal or one concert performance. He received a "salary" of $500 a year. Some years later, it was "raised" to $600, then $750.

Some of the most prominent musicians of the past forty years and more began their training in orchestral work under Arnold Volpe in this organization. Today, all over America, are organizations that are the cultural heirs of this first student orchestra in the United States.

I need not stress how this has enriched the nation, nor tell how to find these organizations patterned after the pioneering YMSO. You have only to listen today . . . in the conservatories

. . . in the thousands of public and private schools . . . in the higher institutions of learning.

As I pass such places and hear the busy rehearsal music pouring from the windows, I feel they are playing a memorial to those days when Arnold first organized the Young Men's Symphony Orchestra.

An especially notable concert of the YMSO marked the tenth anniversary of its founding. Arnold arranged it as a public demonstration, attended by scores of musicians who owed their start in the profession to the YMSO.

Arnold made a speech in which he expressed his thanks to Mr. Seligman by saying, "Mr. Seligman's generous backing and personal interest have inspired the development of orchestral music, not only in this city, but throughout the country."

Already in other American communities, the "Young Men's Symphony Orchestra" was being copied. The idea might have spread even more rapidly had there been more concerts given by the YMSO in its early days. Arnold knew that the concerts, in addition to the inspiration they gave the musicians, attracted the attention of music patrons, music critics and educators.

Among those who understood this was Henry B. Harris. When about to sail for Europe, he donated the use of the Hudson Theatre for the tenth anniversary concert. The program was changed drastically just before it began. Popper's *Requiem* was added. It was performed by three 'cellos in memory of the friends of music who had been lost on the *Titanic*. Among those who perished was Mr. Harris.

One of the 'cellists in this trio was Alfred Seligman—in his last public appearance with the YMSO. Soon the orchestra was playing another memorial concert in the Hudson Theatre, for Mr. Seligman. He had been killed in an automobile accident at West End Avenue and Seventy-second Street.

Arnold considered him a splendid example of democracy in the field of music. Although a man of wealth

WHAT A CARTOONIST SAW AT THE MELLA MARS RECEPTION

...der that critics, newspapermen, pro...ssional musicians, actors and others ...t fall under the mystic spell of Mella ..., the Viennése *diseuse* whom Col. ...rt E. Johnston is introducing to America, a reception was arranged for her on Thursday afternoon of last week at the Hotel Knickerbocker in New York. The New York *World* had one of its cartoonists in attendance and while the results of his visit, reproduced above, are by no means complimentary to the subjects, here and there will be found a characteristic touch to identify the celebrity pictured even without the appended caption.

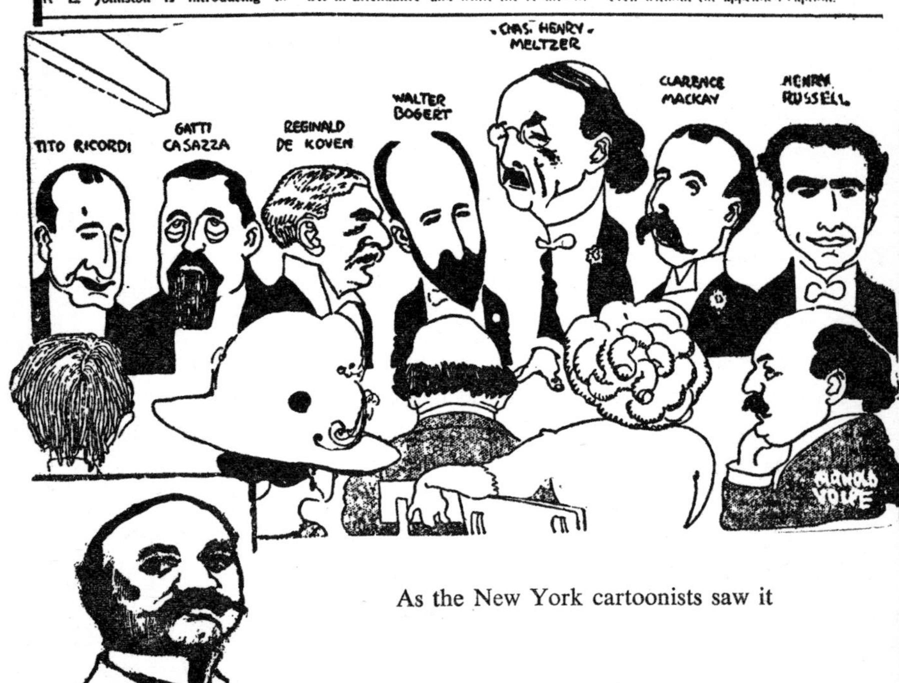

As the New York cartoonists saw it

and high social position, he mingled freely with the young men at the rehearsals. As they became competent to pass the examinations of the Musicians' Union, he frequently loaned them the necessary $100 admission fee. On gala occasions, he invited the entire orchestra and other friends to a banquet.

But in all his kindly deeds, Arnold said, Mr. Seligman was so extremely modest that the world never knew half of his philanthropy.

After Mr. Seligman's death, the finances of the orchestra passed into the hands of the Young Men's Symphony Orchestra Society, of which he had been president and to which his will left money in trust. Over the years, the texture of the orchestra changed. By 1919, the YMSO was no longer composed mainly of amateurs. The members, although young, were serious in their intent to go on as full professionals. The change raised the question of giving concerts.

In previous years, Arnold had pressed the Board of the Society into permitting a number of public performances, first at the Belasco Theatre, then Terrace Garden, and in larger auditoriums. These concerts had been successful. In the light of this proof of ability, Arnold put up to the Board the proposition of establishing a series of concerts on a firm basis.

The Board differed with Arnold. Or, shall we say that Arnold, speaking on behalf of the members of the orchestra, differed with the Board. In order to inform modern readers interested in musical organizations of the past and present, I bring forth from the Arnold Volpe collection of historical documents the exchange of opinions on a point of controversy in 1919. Such differences on artistic matters are by no means unknown in our time.

The question was: Should an orchestra of young musicians, aspiring to professional careers, include in their over-all training a series of public appearances? In April, 1919, Arnold wrote the Board:

"After seventeen years of activity, the YMSO has now passed the experimental stage. The need and usefulness of the organization has long been acknowledged, its success established, and its standards raised from year to year.

"Its membership no longer consists of boys and amateurs content to play without an objective, but of earnest and ambitious young professionals whose sole desire is to rehearse works of the highest order with a view to their performance in public.

"Seeing the need of an incentive to sustained interest in their work, I, in the face of much opposition, inaugurated the concerts at Aeolian Hall four years ago.

"Their instant success definitely proved that this was a step in the right direction and that the concerts, therefore, should be a consistent feature of the work of the orchestra. I do not feel that the Directors are incurring any financial responsibility in giving these concerts as, if properly organized, they could become an asset, as well as a credit to the Society. By 'properly organized' I understand:

"1. They should be given under the auspices of the Society and not dependent on the sale of tickets by the young men.

"2. That adequate advertising be done to bring them to the notice of the public.

"3. To assure satisfactory performances, the number of rehearsals should be increased as may be considered necessary by the conductor."

Arnold brought up an additional point: "In the past, the Directors have not contributed by any personal endeavor to the increase of the endowment fund, but have permitted a false sense of economy to prevail, to the consequent detriment of the artistic growth of the Society. Subscriptions should not be limited to certain private individuals, friends of the late Mr. Seligman, but the general public should also be invited to subscribe to the concerts."

That was the way Arnold saw the situation. He was always

interested in wider participation of the public in musical events and activities. The YMSO had truly progressed beyond its pioneering days. Times had indeed changed, and this change was evident, not only in the texture of the orchestra itself, but in the whole musical realm in New York—thank goodness!

But the Board thought otherwise. I quote from the reply of Severo Mallet-Prevost, the eminent Broad Street attorney, who was president of the Board:

"1. The Board is of the opinion that the concerts should be given as heretofore, not through the Society's invitation, but as the result of the efforts of the young men of the orchestra. The reasons for this are two:

"In the first place, it should be pointed out that the young men are receiving very valuable tuition for which they pay nothing beyond the $1.00 registration fee. Charity, when it is unaccompanied by any effort on the part of the recipient, is nearly always a bad thing.

"The benefit of such charity depends, to a large extent, upon the attitude on the part of the person who is helped, and that attitude is determined, very largely, by the measure of cooperation which the recipient may contribute.

"The concerts are given for the benefit of the young men: they furnish an opportunity to them to contribute to the success of the Society either by buying tickets, or by selling them to their friends. We feel very strongly that this relation of the young men to the concerts should continue; and the Board will take measures to have these views presented to the orchestra next fall, and to see to it that there is a more hearty cooperation on their part.

"Another very important consideration in this connection is that the Society was founded by Mr. Alfred L. Seligman for a very specific purpose, namely, to give young men an opportunity, through practice, to become skillful in orchestral work.

"Mr. Seligman did not contemplate the giving of public concerts, and during his lifetime, very few were given, and even those were for special reasons, applicable to each occasion . . . .

"2. The Board has decided not to advertise the concerts....

"3. The Board has no objection to your increasing the number of rehearsals as much as you wish — provided the Society shall not be called upon to increase its expenses in that connection beyond some additional small sum for the rent of Terrace Garden Hall. Mr. Blomberg thought that this expense would probably not exceed $30.00 for the year."

Spoken like an excellent lawyer! It was indeed an example of charity with plenty of references to the *status quo,* as well as the fact that the Board in 1919 was still putting ditto marks under the views of Alfred Seligman, expressed in 1902.

The real question was whether the Board that controlled the destiny of the YMSO would change with the times or whether its thinking was static and its views outmoded.

It was no more possible for Arnold Volpe's thinking to remain static than for the Board to call Alfred Lincoln Seligman from the grave to ask him in 1919 whether he held the same views as in 1902.

Arnold simply thought asking musicians to keep on rehearsing without giving fairly frequent concerts would be like asking a housewife to prepare delicious meals that were never served to any one, or like expecting a football squad to keep on practicing, without playing any games.

Seventeen years of the YMSO had brought about new conditions, and Arnold was endeavoring to keep abreast of them. The Board stood pat, albeit the differences were entirely on the most friendly plane, with feelings of sincere mutual esteem.

But it was somewhat as if the Constitution of the United States, once adopted, could never be amended to meet the needs of the passing years. Arnold resigned as conductor of the Young Men's Symphony Orchestra. On May 26, 1919, he wrote:

"It is with reluctance and only after mature reflection that

I take this decisive step, as an association of seventeen years cannot be lightly severed, but it would be incompatible with my ideas to retain the post."

There was perhaps another divergence of views, *both* sides of which did not appear in the exchange. That word "charity"! Arnold never counted the tremendous amount of time and effort—far beyond what he was paid for—as giving "charity."

Philanthropy it might have been, but not "charity." He didn't feel that aiding the cause of music in America—whether through time, effort, or money—was "charity." His thoughts and his deeds, which rightly won for him the name of a great pioneer, were on a far loftier scale.

Among the documents relating to the Young Men's Symphony Orchestra is a significant letter written to the Editor of the *Musical Courier,* Sept. 13, 1922, about an article entitled "Americanizing Our Symphonies." It said:

"You quote the Chicago papers, which are naturally very partial to the efforts of Chicago. Not that the Chicago Civic Music Association's efforts are to be belittled, but they do not deserve the credit they are given for founding the first student orchestra in America.

"There has existed a student orchestra at Harvard College since about 1808. This is without a doubt the oldest orchestra in America. The Columbia University had a student orchestra in 1898. The writer was connected with this orchestra for nine years, five years in the capacity of conductor, and had the pleasure later of seeing several of its members in important parts in the symphony orchestras of New York City.

"More important than either of these orchestras in the actual preparation of music students to take their places in symphony orchestras, was the Young Men's Symphony Orchestra of New York City, founded about 1900 by Mr. Arnold Volpe, with the backing of Mr. Seligman, a New York banker who was at the same time an amateur 'cellist. Mr. Volpe directed this orchestra for about seventeen years.

"The writer was a member of it for six years. Today I cannot go into any orchestra concerts in New York or any large moving picture house where a symphony orchestra is maintained, without seeing one or more of my former colleagues of the Young Men's Symphony Orchestra playing in the band.

"I have come here to Cincinnati and found them in the Cincinnati Symphony Orchestra, and I know there are others playing in Cleveland and Detroit."

The letter was signed by Burnet C. Tuthill, General Manager of the Cincinnati Conservatory of Music.

Chapter VII
NEW YORK—1904-1913

IF I HAVE LEFT the impression that the finale with the Young Men's Symphony Orchestra was an abysmal disappointment, let me correct it. In concentrating on the history of the YMSO, I was unable to tell of work even more important that Arnold was doing at the same time—the founding of the Volpe Symphony Orchestra, which for a number of reasons played an impressive role in American musical history.

Just two years after Arnold founded the YMSO, a group of young professional musicians came to him. Their contention was that the YMSO took care only of the needs of students. But what of those who had been graduated and were now members of the Musicians' Union?

The only opportunity these young professionals had to play was in theatres, hotels and restaurants. What outlet had they for their desire to play the great works of the masters? No major symphony would engage young musicians without experience. Members of the New York Philharmonic, for example, were almost all imported Germans. American musicians were the outsiders. They could never hope to join these hallowed ranks.

There was more to it than that. Recall, if you will, how few orchestras and symphonic concerts there were in those days. The paucity seems almost unbelievable. As I have said before, the New York Philharmonic gave only eight pairs of concerts, Friday afternoons and Saturday evenings, if I remember correctly, with the musicians paid on the basis of a sharing of proceeds.

The Boston Symphony came down to New York for five pairs—Thursday evenings and Saturday afternoons. The Chicago, Philadelphia, and Cincinnati Symphony orchestras gave a series. The People's Symphony gave concerts at Cooper Union and the Wetzler orchestra gave several performances at Wanamaker's.

Even without comparing the situation with today—how very little symphonic music then existed; moreover, serious music died out every summer in New York, a matter with which I shall also deal later.

Right after the turn of the century was a good time for an energetic, optimistic young conductor to appear on the American scene.

Arnold's success with the YMSO convinced him conducting should be his life work. He was ready to make any sacrifice to do it, and, for a livelihood, to continue teaching. Included in his aims was a desire to introduce American music, as well as musicians—to put an American *composer* on every program, as well as American soloists.

Undoubtedly that seems like a strange point to emphasize. Today, American compositions are played by most orchestras. But not in 1904 when American composers were receiving practically no recognition. Arnold wanted to — and did — change that, as part of his whole plan for the orchestra.

He came to me. Would I, his wife, stand by him and be willing to share the sacrifices in order to give him his chance? Of course. But I was young and in musical matters inexperienced. I felt unqualified to help him make such an important artistic decision.

Of his ability I had no doubt. His musical background was sufficient to handle every musical situation, and I knew that when Arnold Volpe made up his mind to do a certain thing, nothing could stop him. So to clear up his indecision, one way or the other, I suggested he organize the Volpe Symphony Orchestra, give the first concert, and let the music critics bring in the verdict.

Among the critics in those days were Richard Aldrich, the

New York *Times;* W. J. Henderson, the New York *Sun;* Reginald de Koven, the New York *World;* Henry T. Finck, the New York *Evening Post;* Sylvestor Rawling, the New York *Evening World;* Henry Krehbiel, the New York *Tribune;* Charles Henry Meltzer (later Max Smith), the New York *American;* M. Halperson, the New York *Staats-Zeitung;* Emilie Frances Bauer, the New York *Evening Mail;* and Henry Chapin Plummer, the New York *Call.*

The first concert of the Volpe Symphony Orchestra was scheduled to take place in Mendelssohn Hall, Jan. 17, 1905. Along in December, however, the New York *World* published a humorous drawing, accompanied by the following comment:

> Do you ever pass the comfortable red brick Chemists' Club building on Fifty-fifth Street right near Fifth Avenue, on a Sunday morning? Not morning as the milkman knows it, but the comfortable you-ought-to-be-in-church time—say, between 10 and 12.
>
> No? Yes? Well, we are going to tell you whence all those subtle harmonies. You would never suspect the Chemists' Club of sounds, would you?
>
> Odors of essences and acrid aromas of pungent drugs are expected. Well, there is no fragrance of those cast upon the breeze near the Chemists' Club at all, but there is the sound of high faluting harmonies.
>
> Listen, we will tell you a secret! It is the Volpe Symphony Orchestra. It is rehearsing in the big banquet room of the Chemists' Club every Sunday morning between 10 and 12.
>
> The Volpe Symphony is rehearsing for its series of big concerts beginning in January. But that isn't the interesting part.
>
> The interesting part is the enthusiasm of those crazy musicians, for they must be crazy, surely to patiently draw the tail of a horse across the intestines of a cat or to toot on things that go 'toodle, toodle, toodle!'
>
> Mind you, they don't care a cent for real catchy airs like 'Tammany' or 'Wait Till The Sun Shines Nellie' or 'Them Cruel Words I Can't Forget.'
>
> We asked Arnold Volpe, the leader, why this was thusly. Why the Volpe Symphony Orchestra didn't play 'Won't You Come and Spoon With Me?' or 'Give My Regards to Broadway!' and he said it was because they were musicians . . . .

Today, as I read that forty-five-year-old clipping, it has a far different meaning than it did a few weeks before that crucial first concert in 1905. Then, to our tense and serious minds, it seemed just *too* flippant. In our anxiety for a good reception from the public and the press, it did nothing to add to our composure.

Now let me quote from the music critics after the concert. The *Evening Post* said: "One of the surprises of the musical season was the playing of the Volpe Symphony Orchestra in Mendelssohn Hall last night. It plays with delightful animation and rhythmic swing under the inspiring direction of Arnold Volpe. It was really a delight even to a blasé critic, to hear the orchestra play the Tschaikowsky *Serenade for Strings, op. 48;* here was all the life, verve, rapture, abandon, which the Russian music calls for. Safonoff and the Philharmonic could hardly have done better."

Of course, like all young artists, we had eagerly seized the first editions to read the criticisms. I don't believe we ever read any that delighted us more than those first appraisals of the Volpe Symphony Orchestra.

The *Evening Mail* said: "Mr. Volpe and his men provided all that could be asked of a new organization of this nature—strength, energy, hopefulness, evident relish for their work. No critical comment is called for; the function of this present notice is rather to signalize the emergence of this latest musical undertaking into public view. Mr. Volpe conducted with decision, and the programme was well chosen."

The *Evening Sun* said: "Without long hair or calisthenics to distract his audience, Arnold Volpe last evening conducted the first of this season's three Volpe Symphony orchestral concerts in Mendelssohn Hall for a large and demonstrative audience. The very creditable programme included Beethoven's *Symphony No. 2, D Major, op. 36;* Tschaikowsky's *Serenade for String Orchestra, op. 48;* and Dvorak's *Slavonic Dances, op. 46.*

"Although the director did not indulge in enough light gymnastics to suit some of the audience, he showed that he understood his scores, and he led his musicians with pains and skill without any of the gyrations that usually disturb all but the most seasoned players."

The other critics spoke in the same tones of approval, and Louis Edlin, one of Arnold's violin pupils who appeared as soloist, was also well received.

The whole initial reaction—critics, audience, and many discerning musicians who gave unbiased opinions—was unanimous. Here was Arnold's answer—and mine. I pledged my loyal support to his ambition as a conductor and thenceforth worked by his side to help him achieve the highest.

It was not easy to organize an orchestra, even in those days, without an "angel" behind the backdrop. Although the list of our patrons included many prominent music lovers and the number increased from year to year, there were no *guarantors*. We still often had to pay the deficits out of Arnold's earnings as a teacher. He never drew any salary from the Volpe Symphony Orchestra himself in all the ten years of its existence.

In spite of the fact that the orchestra was incorporated, which relieved Arnold of any financial responsibility, at the first rehearsal each fall he would guarantee the members a certain amount for each concert, a promise he never failed to pay, no matter what the sacrifice entailed for him.

His spirit and his objectives in organizing the orchestra were well stated in his own words in an address he gave in 1906:

"The work of musicians with band and orchestra experience is ever becoming more pronounced. My purpose in inaugurating first the YMSO and later the Volpe Symphony Orchestra was aimed directly to start a creative movement to that end. Nearly every year we see the same men in the representative orchestras. How, then, is the young blood to get a foothold? To become eligible, experience in some orchestral organization is required. They must get it somewhere. Where? Only from such bodies as it is my privilege to lead. The concerts are far-reaching, the principle of the two organizations deeply identified with the progress of music in this country."

The critics, throughout the years, supported Arnold's project with generous space before the concerts and a high calibre of criticism later. Time after time, however, critics came to the concerts thinking that since the Volpe Symphony was comprised of young musicians, its performance would be amateurish. No matter how many times the performances corrected this impression, they never seemed to get over their surprise.

Let me quote from a criticism by Reginald de Koven:

"Although music which is quasi-amateur does not generally lie within the province of professional criticism, I went to the concert of the Volpe Symphony Orchestra in Carnegie Hall yesterday to hear a too little-known *Symphony in D Minor,* by that great and also too little-known French composer, Cesar Franck, a master of the art, in all forms of which he worked with a genius and distinction which but now are beginning to be generally recognized. Cesar Franck brought to music a new element—that of mysticism . . . ."

Then de Koven went on to describe the merits of Franck's music in great detail, such as would be completely unnecessary today. These values, he said, "were well realized by Volpe's capable and sympathetic reading and by the excellent work of the orchestra.

"There was indeed nothing amateurish about their playing, which was marked by a buoyancy and forceful enthusiasm, by a balance and flexibility of tone and smooth compact sonority, and by an excellence of finish in phrasing and nuance which older organizations might envy, and which I must confess, surprised me. But I gladly express my appreciation of the artistic work of both Mr. Volpe and the orchestra."

Arnold was very much appreciated by the critics, not only for his conducting, but for the pioneering work he was always doing, such as helping Cesar Franck's works to become known

Safonoff and his family

Carl Goldmark
Eugene Ysaye (right)

de Coppet Quartet, 1900-1902—Max Karger, Arnold Volpe, Jacob Altschuler Modest Altschuler

de Coppet Quartet, 1902—Alfred Pochon, John Spargur, William Ebann, Arnold Volpe to the public, and for emphasizing the works of American composers.

The effect of his decision on his career was made very clear to me on a memorable occasion. When Glazounov, one of Arnold's greatest inspirations while studying composition in St. Petersburg, came to New York, Arnold was eager to see him and have him meet me. Intentionally, to make it a surprise, Arnold did not have us announced before we went to Glazounov's room in the Ansonia Hotel. It had been thirty years since he had seen Arnold.

As we entered, Glazounov was seated at a table, writing. When he looked up, without a second's hesitation he exclaimed, "Volpe!" and came forward with outstretched arms. Arnold was deeply touched by this immediate recognition and very warm reception. Glazounov was anxious to hear all about Arnold's work. He was disappointed that he had not written any great works, but he fully understood, when Arnold told him he had made conducting his life work. At this Glazounov expressed approval and delight.

Soon after establishment of the Volpe Symphony Orchestra its members were engaged at good salaries by the major symphonies, including the New York Philharmonic. Many of them, as Arnold predicted, held first chairs in all sections and many achieved careers of distinction. Harry Weisbach, Arnold's "discovery," became concertmaster of the Chicago Symphony Orchestra, a position he held for nine years. Mishakoff was another fine violinist. Richard Burgin, now concertmaster and assistant conductor of the Boston Symphony Orchestra, caused a stir in 1907.

The New York *World* reported the incident: "Richard Burgin, the boy violinist, who is a few months less than sixteen years old, was not permitted to play at the Volpe Symphony Orchestra concert last night, nor will he be permitted to play tonight, the Gerry Society having come to the front with the announcement that the violinist is under age. Should he appear on any public stage his arrest will follow . . . .

"Justice Wyatt told the youthful musician, however, that if he attempted to play at the concert last night the Children's Society would get him. The boy appeared at the concert, however, and expected to play.

"He was told by Mr. Volpe to go home, and he burst into tears."

Paul Berthoud became an eminent orchestra personnel manager and was Arnold's personal representative in New York. His devotion to Arnold was that of a son. He came as a violin student in 1906 and progressed through the YMSO to the Volpe Symphony Orchestra. In 1908, he and Arnold went to Europe together, adding to their many delightful experiences a dinner with Mr. and Mrs. de Coppet, their daughter Pauline, and Kurt Schindler at their villa in Switzerland, and another with the Flonzaley Quartet in their studio at Gourse Canon de Vaud. They also went together to see Carl Goldmark.

Years after, when Howard Barlow had become musical director for the Columbia Broadcasting System, he recounted to me an experience as a youngster under Arnold. Howard at that time was interested more in reading scores than in watching the conductor. At rehearsal, his eyes were so absorbed by the score that he didn't come in on time.

"There was no mercy shown," he recalled, laughing. "The 'old man' threw me out of the orchestra."

Arnold went to one of Howard's broadcasts later and was very proud of his "boy."

Once Mark Warnow—long after he had become a popular radio conductor—asked me if I remembered a young violin student who always came at least an hour early for his lesson and sat in our living room by the studio door. I told him: "Of course, I remember. How could I forget? You don't mean to say you were *that* boy—*that* nuisance."

His answer was most touching. "Yes," he said, "it was *this* boy. I just had to come early. I wanted to breathe the wonderful atmosphere of your home—the peace and joy I experienced nowhere else—to talk with those lovely daughters—to be near the man who was not only my teacher, but my inspiration. What an influence he was throughout my life!"

The joys of working with those "boys" can never be measured. They came eagerly asking for artistic training, and Arnold gave so freely of himself. He was glad that in America it was possible, and glad that none of them had to stand freezing on the doorstep awaiting permission from the governor to enter.

One of Arnold's thoughtful considerations for his pupils was his exact scheduling of lessons. His own personal experiences as a pupil had been to wait for hours outside the studio. He felt it was the duty of teachers to arrange their teaching schedules so that students would not have to undergo tense, long waiting. This he did successfully.

Here is but a brief list of musicians who received their sound early training from Arnold, either with the Young Men's Symphony or the Volpe Symphony Orchestra. I regret that after so many years many of the names—which ran into the hundreds—I can not remember. Here are just a few who made outstanding careers:

Mark Warnow, Nat Schildkret, Walter Kramer, Louis Edlin, Henry van Praag, Burnet C. Tuthill, Nat Finston, Max Meth, Max Rabinoff, Samuel Lifshey, George King Raudenbush, Leon Barzin, Benjamin Kohon, Max Jacobs and Harry Weisbach.

Chapter VIII

VOLPE SYMPHONY "BOYS"

LET ME GIVE you Arnold's own definition of a conductor:

"To be a conductor of an orchestra means, not only to be a thorough musician, but also to have the quality that reaches and holds every individual member, to get the best work out of each one and make him feel, not only his own responsibility as an individual, but also as a part of the entire unit."

How successfully Arnold lived up to this definition was revealed on an occasion I shall never forget. By the end of the first five years, the Volpe Symphony Orchestra had attained a recognition that many older organizations might have envied.

The public, the world of professional musicians, the newspapers and the musical press were all in agreement as to its lofty achievements. Arnold, nevertheless, was not conducting the orchestra for *their* benefit. An abiding question prodded his mind: "What is this doing for 'my boys'?"

At the end of that memorable fifth season, "his boys" told him very clearly. While the rest of the orchestra applauded thunderously, David Kulinyi came forward and said:

"Mr. Volpe, on behalf of the members of the Volpe Symphony Society of last season, I wish to present to you these busts. (At this point David handed him, one by one, three magnificent bronze busts of Beethoven, Wagner and Liszt.) I am sure that you need no introduction to them. Their commercial value may not be very great, yet in selecting these great composers as conveyors of our respect, our gratitude, and our good wishes toward you, we beg of you always to bear in mind that as great as these men were, just so great are our good wishes for your success in the future, whether with the Volpe Symphony Society or elsewhere.

"I am sure all the members join me in congratulating you upon the artistic success of last season, and we all hope the coming one will be as great financially as the last one was artistically.

"May these busts always remind you of us, the members of the Volpe Symphony Society of 1908-1909, and may you and your family live in the best of health to look upon them for many, many years."

In reporting the event, the *Musical Courier* noted that Arnold made "a graceful response" to Mr. Kulinyi's "happy speech" and that the season "ended in a shout of joy, and with the brightest prospects ahead."

The *Courier* went on to say: "The educational importance of the Volpe movement is attracting notice even outside of New York. Many men and women of wealth are interested, and no one need feel surprised, when the time comes, to announce that the institution has been placed on a permanent basis."

This was the season, too, when Albert Spalding, the violinist, made his first appearance with the Volpe Symphony. It was his second American appearance. I smile as I note in that old clipping of 1909 that he made only the second headlines. But here is what a critic said further down:

"The real sensation of the evening was the reception accorded young Albert Spalding, the American violinist, who has taken such a strong hold on music-lovers of this city in his first season."

The fact that Arnold was destined to work closely with so many young people resulted in his having many "contemporaries" who, all his life, as long as he knew them, were in delightful, vigorous ascendancy, when each year brought them new maturity of personality and artistry, higher joys, and greater triumphs.

There were so many of these superior young artists with whom we formed lifelong friendships—so many that I can not now justly take space to name them *all.* I have already named some, and there were also Rudolph Ganz who appeared with the orchestra in 1908, Maximilian Pilzer in 1910, Rosina and Josef Lhevinne, Clara Butt and Efrem Zimbalist in 1913, and many others. My sister, Henriette Michelson, the pianist, appeared with the orchestra several times.

The Volpe Symphony Orchestra played a special historic program at the Wanamaker Auditorium, May 22, 1913, the centenary celebration of Richard Wagner's birth, when a bust was unveiled.

Not all of the soloists with the orchestra were young. There are wonderful memories of Anton Hekking, the eminent 'cellist. After his appearance with the orchestra, we went to his hotel room and there, by dim light, he played for us far into the early hours. I can never forget in this storehouse of memory, to which there seems no limit, Gerardy the 'cellist.

Because Arnold gave so much time and attention to the accompaniments for soloists, they loved appearing with him. Usually he would have at least one private rehearsal, in order to become acquainted with the artists' tempi and interpretations. This he considered the secret of a conscientious director.

Most of the private rehearsals took place in his studio in our home, giving me a chance to meet the artists on a more intimate footing. After the rehearsal, they would usually dine with us. One amusing instance of 1908 comes to mind.

Dr. Ludwig Wullner, the lieder singer, and Coenraad Bos came to rehearse. Dr. Wullner was soon to recite *Das Hexenlied (The Witch's Song)* with the orchestral setting composed by Max Schillings. During the entire dinner he was very nervous, clasping his hands to his heart and exclaiming, "Mein Herz!" (My heart!)

He would turn to Mr. Bos and say: "Wir mussen Morgen zum Doctor gehen." (We must go to the doctor tomorrow.)

Mr. Bos would wink at us and reply: "Ja, ja, Morgen gehen wir." (Yes, yes, tomorrow we will go.)

It was to be Dr. Wullner's first American appearance, and this was just stage fright, although well in advance of the concert.

There were so many fine individuals who deserve to be mentioned with highest praise for their help with the Volpe Symphony Orchestra. Their interest and aid was an important and real part of the movement to aid young musicians toward further careers.

Mrs. George H. Kendall, whose husband was President of the New York Bank Note Company, acted as treasurer for years. Others who came forward were Otto Bauer, Mrs. Lawson Purdy, Mrs. Le Roy Dresser, Dr. Lewis O'Bryan and Mrs. Henry Clarke Coe.

One who made a generous and unforgettable contribution to the Volpe Symphony Society was Louise Volpe, our English cousin. She was the wife of Maurice Volpe, Arnold's cousin who had lived most of his life in Paris. Louise Volpe's command of English was phenomenal. Her mind was an encyclopedia, and during the ten years of the orchestra, as our volunteer secretary, she helped enthusiastically in every possible way.

A most generous supporter was E. J. de Coppet who, as a great patron of music, reserved his due right to make gifts in his own way. He once wrote Arnold: "I have received a letter from a Mrs. Kendall thanking me for a check she says is to be given to a fund for your orchestra. Now, I must tell you that such was not my intention when I mailed you the check.

"My present was a tribute to you personally, to your work and your ability as shown at the last concert. If you desire to turn the amount over to a fund, you can of course do as you please, but it must appear there as *your* gift."

It was handled according to Mr. de Coppet's wishes, and it paid the deficit for the season.

The following is another letter from Mr. de Coppet which Arnold always treasured:

314 West Eighty-fifth Street

Dear Mr. Volpe—

Thank you for sending me the box for last night's concert. The latter was *excellent*. There is, to me, a freshness and an artistic earnestness in your band of young men, which I do not find in any other orchestra in New York. As to your own artistic worth, it shone brightly thro' the whole evening. I have never enjoyed Tschaikowsky's symphony as I did yesterday. But what gave me most pleasure was the Beethoven overture. You know that I go rarely to concerts nowadays; but if you play a Beethoven symphony next winter I shall not fail to attend. Mr. Stahlberg's composition seemed to me very interesting. I should however wish to know it better, before daring to express an opinion as to its worth.

With my hearty congratulations I remain

Sincerely yours,
E. J. de Coppet

New York - March 27th/08

Our friendship with Albert Spalding and with his parents, Mr. and Mrs. J. W. Spalding, grew during many delightful week-ends at their lovely home in Monmouth Beach, New Jersey. There was marvelous food prepared by their skilled Italian cook and always a great deal of chamber music.

During World War II, Spalding laid aside his violin and, using his excellent knowledge of the Italian tongue and people, became an anonymous voice over a clandestine radio station, communicating with partisans behind the lines who helped in the eventual liberation. It was a dangerous "cloak and dagger" job.

There are so many sides to the character of a musician. Arnold, for example, never appeared to his audiences to be the strict taskmaster he was during rehearsals. He was honest, however, in being equally strict with himself and working just as hard as he asked his musicians to do.

Out of Arnold's exceptional amount of work with young musicians came one thing especially that brought him much notice. He did not use scores while conducting. For a long time, he and Toscanini were among the very few conductors who could do this.

The press and the public frequently remarked about it. He did not lay scores aside for the effect or as a publicity stunt. In working so much with young people he had to give them each entrance cue. The scores were in his way. Besides, he knew every score from cover to cover, and eventually he came to wonder how a conductor, with his eyes buried in the score, could be free to give all his attention to musical interpretation.

In the total of all the reasons for his success in working with young people, there was far more, however, than his great musical gift.

At the last concert of the Young Men's Symphony Orchestra in 1919, for example, I had as my guest that eminent composer and musician, Ernest Bloch. The program included Brahms *Symphony No. 2 in D Major.*

At the end, Mr. Bloch turned to me and said: "There is nothing like this in the whole of Europe."

Later, when he and Arnold met in Los Angeles, Mr. Bloch described his experiences with the YMSO and wanted to know how he, Arnold, could have given such a performance with such material.

W. J. Henderson, music critic for the New York *Sun,* remarked: "Mr. Volpe's success in transforming raw musical material into a working orchestra must indubitably be recognized."

It was simply that Arnold, in addition to his musicianship, had an ability to conjure miracles out of young and inexperienced players. He had great patience, a true understanding and love of youth. Most of all, he was willing to forget himself in helping others.

This continuous interest in the welfare of others, I believe, caused him to be a pioneer in another phase of music. Whenever the full history of American musical composition is written, Arnold will occupy a prominent place in it.

He considered the recognition of American composers as the final stage in our country's musical education and development. Despite his lack of an endowed institution to defray the costs of the necessary additional rehearsals for new works, he consistently endeavored to further an appreciation of native American compositions by including them in his programs.

He never refused to look at new scores. In his evaluation of new works, he was severe but honest and, most of the time, right.

His advice to young composers, either as suggestions to seek success in some other field or as encouragement to continue writing, was a real help to many.

Perhaps the best way to tell of his help to composers is to list here some of the works and the dates on which he presented them to audiences.

RESUME OF WORKS OF AMERICAN COMPOSERS AND COMPOSERS LIVING IN AMERICA PERFORMED BY THE VOLPE SYMPHONY ORCHESTRA AT CARNEGIE HALL

April 14, 1907

Tone Poems Op. 22 — *MacDowell*
(a) Hamlet
(b) Ophelia
Repeated Jan. 8, 1911

March 26, 1908

Symphonic Suite—Uebers Weltenmeer — *Fritz Stalberg*
First Performance

Dec. 4, 1910

Overture Macbeth — *Stillman-Kelley*
First Performance
Repeated at Central Park August 24, 1913

Feb. 12, 1911

The Domain of Hurakan — *Arthur Farwell*
First Performance
Played twice at Central Park August 10, 1924

March 19, 1911

Two Movements from Suite in D minor — *Arthur Foote*

March 28, 1911		
	Christmas Overture First Performance	*Percy Goetchius*
Jan. 9, 1912		
	Symphony in D minor First Performance	*Pietro Floridia*
March 26, 1912		
	Piano Concerto in D minor Played by Leo Ornstein	*MacDowell*

PERFORMED AT CENTRAL PARK, N. Y.

July 11, 1912		
	Southern Fantasie Repeated Aug. 26, 1913	*W. H. Humiston*
July 11, 1912		
	Overture—Russia	*Platon Brounoff*
Aug. 26, 1913		
	Tone Poem—Hamlet	*MacDowell*
	Theme and Variations, Suite op. 30	*Foote*
	Overture—Cornell	*Arthur Farwell*
Aug. 7, 1913		
	Overture—In Bohemia	*Henry Hadley*
Aug. 20, 1913		
	Gaelic March	*Stillman-Kelley*
	Scherzo	*Ernest Carter*

PERFORMED AT LEXINGTON OPERA HOUSE

Sept. 1, 1912		
	Intermezzo from opera, "The Galleon"	*James P. Dunn*

Chapter IX
HOME LIFE

ALTHOUGH our home life was a mingling of family life and the demands of a musician's career, we never lived as Bohemians.

Arnold has sometimes been described as a man who would always arrive at rehearsals at least an hour early, but for dinner would often be late. It was true that his concentration on his work made him more than punctilious in the studio and the rehearsal halls all his life. But our domestic life was not entirely unscheduled.

It began running on a normal routine soon after we were married, despite Arnold's previous habits of bachelorhood. There were exigencies caused by the nature of his work, of course, but we agreed that he had his work to do, and I had mine—the running of the home. The two went on concurrently with smooth regularity.

No man ever expressed greater love or devotion to a woman than Arnold to me. His great tenderness to me during two illnesses helped me more than all the doctors in the world could have done. During one of them, when we lived in Far Rockaway, he would travel every day at noon from New York to walk with me around the block and then return to his studio. When I went through a more serious experience in 1923, the Bible was his constant companion, praying me back to health.

Although I always remained first in his thoughts and consideration, fatherhood brought great happiness to Arnold. Our cup ran over with joy when, at the end of the first year, our first-born child, Eleanor, came to us, February 19, 1903. She was a beautiful baby.

Our equally beautiful second baby, Cecilia, was born

three years later, on November 20, 1906.

Even in the early days of the twentieth century, when child-rearing at least was supposed to be conducted by sterner rules than today, I was pointed out as an example. When my daughter Eleanor was but nine-and-a-half, she told me I was the most talked-about woman in the neighborhood. When I asked her why, she replied: "Oh, 'cause you don't let Ceci and me do any of the things the other girls do."

My answer was: "That's all right, Eleanor, but do you know any other little girls as strong and well as you are?"

When a newspaper, about that time, was making a good deal of a doctor's assertion that "the American mother needs to go to school to learn her job," Marguerite Mooers Marshall came to interview me and meet the children. I was pleased when, after seeing the girls and inquiring my methods, she wrote:

"Do you know who is the healthiest, wholesomest, most generally-satisfactory child in New York? The quintessence of childhood as it should be may assuredly be found in the person of little Miss Eleanor Volpe. She has the firm, apple-red cheeks, the dark eyes glowing like frost sparkles, the square, sturdy, splendidly-resistant figure of the normal country child who, I thought, had disappeared with the little red schoolhouse." Because Eleanor was the older, she spoke more of her as an example of my results, but she could have been equally complimentary of Cecilia.

Every day I was up at half-past six, giving my children their baths. I ate every meal with them when they were young. I took them to school in the morning, went after them at noon, took them back at one o'clock and went for them at three.

They had their supper at half-past five, and Cecilia went to bed at half-past six. Eleanor went to bed at half-past seven. In those earlier days, the children never went to the theatre or to a moving-picture show. They did not go to dancing school until much, much later. They never wore elaborate clothes, and spending money was allowed only on rarest occasions.

I believed the great principle in bringing up children was to keep their lives simple, and to fill them with the natural duties and pleasures of childhood. I loved my children devotedly, and I would do anything in the world for their comfort and well-being. But over-indulgence I considered the most cruel sort of kindness.

I was sixteen when I first went to the opera. It was the most marvelous experience in the world. I wanted my daughters to know such keen and perfect joy. If they were taken to the theatre before they were old enough to understand and appreciate what they saw, all the freshness and glamour would be worn off before they reached the age of appreciation. I felt this about all amusements that were artificial for children.

The most pitiable being on earth, I thought, was the blasé, self-conscious child. The supreme charm of childhood is naturalness. How could they be natural if they were dressed up and shown off like mechanical toys? The parent should not break the will of the child, but should control it. What nonsense to say the parent does not know more than the immature, little being confided to its care. My children were not permitted to think themselves superior to an older person.

Despite my stern-sounding principles, I assure you, there was nothing timid or woebegone about our daughters. They scampered and played, and were obviously happy—and healthy.

Since Arnold's studio was nearly always in the same house, we had all our noon meals together. Because our children were natural and gay, they were the delight of many guests, who came frequently to dine with us. The children were not allowed at the evening dinner table until their twelfth year, but they often appeared briefly at tea.

The reaction one afternoon of the Russian, Safonoff, conductor of the New York Philharmonic, gave us an amusing family incident. When he met the children, he turned to Arnold and said:

"I knew you were a fine musician, but I didn't know you were also a great sculptor. Any more?"

Arnold answered, "No, two, that's all."

The following day we received from Safonoff an inscribed photograph of himself and his wife—and beside them, in a long, descending row, their *eight* children.

Eleanor's childish pranks one time gave her a memory of Eugene Ysaye. He and his son Gabriel often came to play in quartets. He was large and portly and had an extreme fondness for cider—just plain, sweet cider. His capacity for this beverage, I found when I endeavored to stock the house with enough to satisfy him, was enormous.

As we went in to dinner one evening, Eleanor trailed Ysaye, walking with her cheeks puffed out and her stomach stuck forward, in caricature of his rotundity. He turned and saw her. She was frightened and embarrassed at being caught in the act. But how he laughed—peals of laughter—and catching her up in his great arms, patted her, with tears of merriment rolling down his cheeks.

During their father's busy summer months, as the children grew older, they enjoyed camp life in the Catskill Mountains with its freedom and association with children of their own ages under right supervision. They were not allowed to go out unchaperoned in the evenings until their eighteenth birthdays. In this, I may have been overstrict.

And, too, they missed witnessing many of their father's successes—unless the concerts were in the afternoon. I regret this, but they were by no means deprived of hearing good music in public. We had boxes for all the matinee performances at the Metropolitan Opera House and for the symphony concerts, as soon as they reached an age of appreciation.

Many parties and late afternoon dances were held for them and their schoolmates at home. They also had the pleasure of meeting the many artists who came to dine, although they were not present during the entire evening.

Eleanor was gifted, and she began to study the piano at the age of six, with some of the best teachers in New York. But because she was such a good sight reader, she was tempted to avoid practice. She was talented also in drawing and with the needle. Quite early she made her own dresses.

Cecilia begged her father to teach her violin. He refused, saying it was too difficult an instrument to play well. He hoped that neither daughter would become a professional musician —or marry one. He had his wish. Cecilia had a charming small voice and excelled in aesthetic dancing.

As the girls grew older, the four of us had much fun together at home in many musical hours. Eleanor would be at the piano, with Arnold playing the violin. I would be singing, with Cecilia prompting me with all the words I had a hard time to remember.

When Arnold tried his hand at writing a musical comedy for a libretto by Milton Goldsmith, each evening the girls would ask to hear the latest number. They sat around the piano and criticized, until eventually they knew every word and note of the entire work. When they tired of this, they would teach their father the newest dance steps.

Our elder daughter was married June 4, 1924, to Morris Dreyfus, of Kansas City. It was not a happy marriage. For fourteen years we hoped it would work out, but on a visit to us in Florida, she opened her heart and told us she would not go back to her husband. They were divorced July 7, 1938. Her father took it very hard. The marriage bond was a sacred one to him, and the thought of divorce was unpleasant. I am glad that Arnold lived to see his first-born married again to an old schoolmate.

She is now Mrs. Labori Krass of Rochester, New York. Her husband is a prosperous merchant and a graduate of Columbia University, where he and Eleanor first knew each other. They

At right, Diploma from the Imperial Russian Musical Society, St. Petersburg Conservatory, signifying that Arnold Volpe "graduated in Harmony and Counterpoint with high standing and marked success. Outstanding in Canon and Fugues."—April 24, 1897.

Below: Diploma from the Warsaw University, 1886.

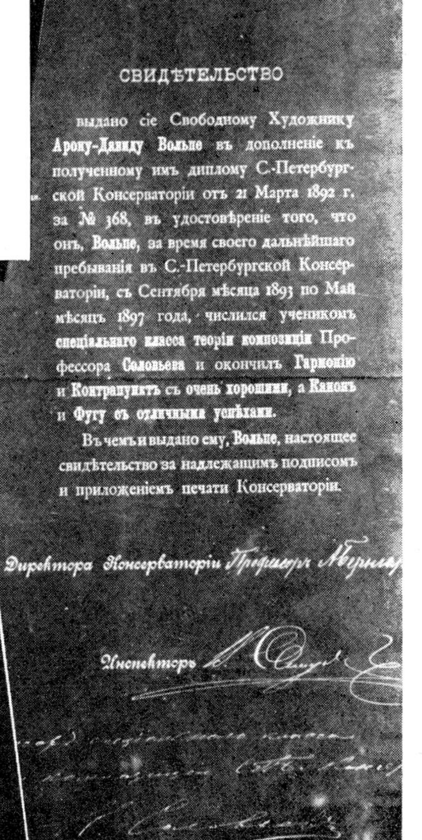

СВИДѢТЕЛЬСТВО

выдано сіе Свободному Художнику Арону-Давиду Вольпе въ дополненіе къ полученному имъ диплому С.-Петербургской Консерваторіи отъ 21 Марта 1892 г. за № 368, въ удостовѣреніе того, что онъ, Вольпе, за время своего дальнѣйшаго пребыванія въ С.-Петербургской Консерваторіи, съ Сентября мѣсяца 1893 по Май мѣсяцъ 1897 года, числился ученикомъ спеціальнаго класса теоріи композиціи Профессора Соловьева и окончилъ Гармонію и Контрапунктъ съ очень хорошими, а Канонъ и Фугу съ отличными успѣхами.

Въ чемъ и выдано ему, Вольпе, настоящее свидѣтельство за надлежащимъ подписомъ и приложеніемъ печати Консерваторіи.

Директора Консерваторіи Профессоръ

Инспекторъ

Professor Leopold Auer

"To my beloved and talented pupil Arnold Volpe with much affection."—Solovieff were married January 26, 1939. Ernestine, Eleanor's beautiful daughter by her first marriage, was born September 17, 1931. Ambitious to become a singer, she is in her junior year at Connecticut College for Women.

Our younger daughter, Cecilia, is now Mrs. Jerome M. Joffee, of Kansas City. Her husband is an attorney. They have three children: Lenore, born December 7, 1929, a graduate of the class of '50 of the University of Miami, from which her mother was graduated; Jerome, Jr., born October 11, 1936; and Arnold Volpe Joffee, born December 24, 1942. As the second Arnold Volpe, this youngest grandchild resembles his grandfather, remarkably duplicating Arnold's sturdy, stocky physique.

Lenore is a gifted musician. At the age of three, using a quarter-size violin, she started to learn the violin from her grandfather. Arnold considered her the most gifted pupil he had ever had in his entire career. In the summer of 1939, when she came on a visit to Florida, he gave her his own fine Lupot. From the time she was a baby, he would talk chords, scales and intervals with her. He would make her play everything on the piano that she played on the violin and transpose in every key. She has perfect pitch and a keen appreciation of good music.

Our daughters' devotion to us is best expressed in the letters written on their wedding days.

The letter from Arnold to Ceci was written after the announcement of her engagement to Jerome.

The letter to me was written when I went to Kansas City to be with Ceci when her first baby was born.

My own darling Mother and Dad,

I am the most grateful girl in the world—why? I have the most unselfish and wonderful parents on this Earth, I have the most loving and devoted husband in the universe, I have had the most elegant and beautiful wedding that any girl ever dreamed of, and I am the most fortunate girl in the world to have everything that anyone could wish for. I want to remind you that I am and always will be your devoted daughter and want to assure you that my heart is full of appreciation, devotion, love and thanksgiving for a perfectly happy twenty-one years in a harmonious and sympathetic home and environment.

Not loving you less or loving my darling husband more, I will always be your

Most devoted
Eleanor

July 11, 1928

Dearest Ceci,

I must say that the great news about you and Jerome certainly surprised us and naturally quite upset us.

It is hard to realize it for it is so sudden and so unexpected. It is by far the greatest and most important event in your life, an event in which I can plainly see the hand of God. You remember, dear, our conversation about Jerome not so long ago. I told you what I thought of him as a man and what an ideal husband he would make, but I would never believe that he would be so determined and fall for you as he did.

Only a few days ago, when discussing our proposed trip to Europe, Mother remarked that she would so much like to have Ceci go with us, and that she would not leave unless Ceci was perfectly happy and contented, in Kansas City. The events of last week seem to be an answer to her prayers. What a wonderful demonstration! Our hearts are full of joy and pain—the joy of seeing you happy and the pain of parting with you, for I am afraid you will never want to go back to Florida with us, or ever to come to old New York. However, as this is His will, we rejoice with you and pray that God's blessings, guidance and protection be with you both all the days of your lives.

Our plans are still indefinite but we will make up our minds soon about going to Europe. I am sure you will now be taken care of, and in the meantime everything will work out beautifully.

With fondest love to you all including Jerome.

Your
Daddy

I forgot to thank you all for the gorgeous ties. Whoever selected them showed good taste.

October 10, 1928

My darling Mother and Father,

How quickly time flies. I can remember when I was a little girl, how I'd dream of beautiful things and marriage was one. Now my dreams are fulfilled and I am happy—so happy.

But in my great joy, dearest parents, I could not but stop to think of why I am so happy. Why because of you. It was your love, your devotion and your comradeship that made me the girl I am, a girl proud to go to any man, and a girl who was able to get a man as clean as she.

You have been more than wonderful and patient with me. Fear not that I will ever forget you because I am married. I love you both as no other daughter could love her parents. I'll pray for you each day, and my greatest hope is to see you happy and without financial worriment. It will come. Just trust in God. I've learned how and it's wonderful.

God bless you both and keep you well for me, forever. Always your baby girl.

Ceci

Dec. 24, 8 P. M.

Dearest,

This is Christmas eve. I am terribly lonesome but I do not complain. I felt kind of blue all day yesterday. I thought there must be something wrong with Ceci, otherwise you would not have changed your plan to leave on the 22nd. Your letter and telegram cheered me up this morning. I was certainly happy to hear that Ceci is all right and that you have decided to leave on Thursday. I do hope that there will be no disappointment at this time. I doubt whether this letter will reach you, but am taking a chance.

Please don't worry about the length of the program. I figured every number and it is not too long.

I am so happy to think that you will be with me soon again. I do not like to be separated from you even for the shortest time. Believe it or not, but that's the truth. I know you will all have a happy Christmas. My love to you and the children.

Devotedly,
Arnold

At times Arnold's modesty about his composing talent was provoking. One evening, after Dr. Percy Goetchius and Rubin Goldmark had dined with us, the three were in the studio looking over a composition by Dr. Goetchius that the orchestra was soon to perform. In passing the door, I heard them discussing fugues and went in and asked them if they had seen the fugues Arnold had composed as a student. They insisted he show them.

Arnold was annoyed with me, requesting them not to pay any attention to me, and asking me to kindly leave the room.

But they insisted, and were at the piano with the fugues until long after midnight. They were much impressed and Dr. Goetchius asked to take them to show to students.

One of our dinner parties was for Mischa Elman on his twenty-first birthday. Other guests were Pochon, Betti, d'Archambeau and Ara, of the Flonzaley Quartet, and, of course, Papa Elman. As we lingered over the table, Mischa asked for our attention.

Was he right in believing, he asked, now he had become of age, that he should be able to handle his own affairs and travel without his father? We were all taken aback. Up to that day, Papa Elman, as he was affectionately known to the musical world, had been at Mischa's call day and night. Every detail of Mischa's career was arranged and controlled by Papa. One could not think of Mischa without him.

After many constructive suggestions by everyone, it was Papa who, then and there, diplomatically stated that Mischa was right; he would give him free reign to take over the business affairs. In less than two years, however, Mischa asked his father again to accompany him on his tours.

Maria Grever, the Spanish composer, came to us with her two small children in 1918, when we lived on 77th Street. She was lonely and without money, but filled with music and ambition. We took her into our home and into our hearts.

She played and sang some of her first attempts at composition for Arnold—things she had done without even knowing how to read notes. He immediately recognized a great talent for her special type of music, encouraged her to keep on, and predicted a fine future. Later, she studied a great deal, and we rejoiced in her resultant success. To her, Arnold was always "Papa Volpe," and her devotion to both of us continued through the years.

I loved to give surprise parties for Arnold. It was always fun, for he was ever unsuspecting. On one of his birthdays I invited about ten of his "boys" from the orchestra. They came at six in the morning, tiptoeing in, with their shoes in one hand and their instruments in the other. When they were ready to play, I opened his bedroom door, and they awakened him with one of his own compositions.

He sleepily walked out into the room in his pajamas, tears of delight rolling down his cheeks. But the first thing he said was:

"Why didn't you tune up?"

It made me really cross.

"Arnold, how could they?" I reminded. "The tuning would have awakened you and spoiled the surprise."

Then we were all very merry at a breakfast of beefsteak and all the trimmings. The boys stayed until noon.

Musical events were not the only ones on our social calendar. Many prominent artists have a predilection for poker games, and although their ideas of betting limits varied, we would solve this by having different tables according to stakes. Arnold never played higher than a twenty-five-cent limit, although his luck was better than average.

Food in our home consisted largely of Continental dishes. At the beginning of our married life, cooking gave me a problem. Since I had been with my parents in business, I had never had time nor opportunity to learn to cook.

I soon realized Arnold was fond of certain dishes and expected them. From my mother and various members of Arnold's family I got the recipes. It naturally took more than one trial to produce palatable results, but after many repetitions of each opus, the finales became better and better with each performance. Pleasing Arnold was never a matter of finickiness. His preferences were normal and his digestion hearty.

During the first three years of our marriage, we had some pretty good servants, but they were poor cooks. Then came Irma, our Hungarian cook. She stayed with us for sixteen years. How she could cook! And what a tyrant!

Even I feared to go into her kitchen. But what mattered that, when out of it came such artistry in *chicken paprika, wiener schnitzel,* and such *strudel, mandel torte* and *kaffee kuchen!*

What dishes did Arnold like best? Breakfast was always simple: fruit, hot cereal, toast and tea. But when he seemed disturbed or worried, I knew that chicken livers, fried lightly in butter with onions, soothed him.

Our luncheons were usually light—sliced cucumbers, radishes and hardboiled eggs, with *plenty* of sour cream and sometimes cottage cheese.

Or I would fry very thin slices of salami in butter, and when crisp cover them with two well-beaten eggs. He was very fond of this. There was always tea, rye bread, hard rolls and cheese. Imported Swiss was his favorite. Smoked whitefish and lox were his preferred appetizers.

With the tea served in his studio in the afternoon, he enjoyed *kaffee kuchen,* always fresh-baked at home, crunchy outside and dreamily light and airy within.

Some of his favorite dinner dishes were *borscht,* with plenty of sour cream, and a boiled potato. *Blintzes* were served with sour cream, too, and sugar and cinnamon. There was special *gefüllte fish,* which took an hour to prepare from whitefish, carp and pike, and three hours to cook. Hot or cold, it was usually enhanced with horseradish.

Wiener schnitzel, of course, was much enjoyed, and my pot roast with browned potatoes, and almost every kind of fowl. Few of these things were extraordinary in their ingredients, but in their preparation and seasoning there had to be art.

Always when our daughters inquired what we were going to have for dinner, their response seemed to be, "Oh yes, Daddy likes that!" When Arnold heard women complain of difficulties in pleasing their husbands with meals, he would turn to me and say: "You see how lucky you are, Marie. I never complain, do I?"

Then I would have, in truth, to say, "Of course not, because all the meals are planned only for you."

Once, for a period, chicken did not appear on our menu. It was right after the reception we gave Professor Auer. Irma, our cook, agreed to my plan to serve chicken salad, on the promise that Eleanor, Cecilia and I would cut up the chickens, the celery, etc. Since we expected four hundred guests, we started at six o'clock in the morning. At noon, Eleanor stopped and expressed our attitude toward chickens: "Mother, I never want to see another chicken as long as I live."

Arnold's meals just before performances had to be sustaining but light. Usually the menu that met these requirements consisted of broiled lamb chops or chicken, a salad, baked apple and, of course, tea.

We never served hard liquor at our table, and only now and then beer and wine for our guests.

Conducting made Arnold extremely thirsty. I usually had fruit juices ready for him at intermissions. After the strain of a performance, he could drink quarts of water or soft drinks. After either a rehearsal or a concert, the routine also included an alcohol rubdown and a complete change of clothing.

As a violinist, he had long been thoughtful of his fingers and immaculate with them. He rarely ate even a piece of chicken with them, lest he soil them. His hands were as soft as those of a well-groomed woman, with the exception of the hard calluses formed by years of pressure on the violin strings. All of us in the family were so conscious of his hands that we never let him carry even the smallest package.

Yes, in a sense he was spoiled, first by his mother, then by me, then by his children, and in later years by his grandchildren, who adored him and, in true tradition, alertly awaited his homecoming for the privilege of slipping off his shoes and putting on his slippers. All these attentions, however, did not make him selfish or less modest or humble. On the contrary, they drew us all closer together.

Like many Russians, he was very emotional, and his moods

came easily to the surface. He never could hide them from me. If something had not gone according to his liking at rehearsal, or with pupils at the studio, I immediately sensed it. I would make him rest a bit, while I prepared one of his favorite dishes. That usually succeeded in clearing the atmosphere and bringing a smile to his face again, and I soon learned which dishes were the best antidotes.

Chapter X

CENTRAL PARK—1909-1913

ARNOLD was busy during the winter season conducting the Young Men's Symphony Orchestra, the Volpe Symphony Orchestra, and the Orchestra of the Brooklyn Institute of Arts and Sciences. At the invitation of Professor Franklin W. Hooper, he had started conducting the Institute's orchestra for training young men, in 1909. He continued for nine years, through 1918, adding to his store of pleasant memories, for numerous talented boys were discovered, among them Benno Rabinoff.

The year 1910 was especially memorable. I recall a friend asking me years later, "What were you doing in 1910?"

I was looking after Arnold and the children, I told her—the usual. Arnold, however, I pointed out, was doing something historic. When I explained he was conducting orchestral concerts in Central Park, my friend didn't seem to recognize it as at all unusual. How perfectly natural it was of her to assume that orchestral music was always a part of the scene in New York's great parks. To witness the beginning of fine music in the Park was thrilling, for it was truly an experiment. There were many doubters.

In the spring of 1910, one of the first directors of the Brooklyn Institute of Arts and Sciences, Gregory Weinstein, a friend interested in all cultural developments, asked Arnold to confer with Charles B. Stover, Park Commissioner for the City of New York.

New York was about to enter upon what the music critics of the day called the "silly season," since serious music died out in the spring. All summer, the music-loving public was offered no more substantial fare than resounding marches and light waltzes played by bands. Dock Commissioner Tompkins and Commissioner Stover presented similar programs on the municipal recreation piers and in the parks.

Arnold, of course, was always at odds with those in power who held that the public was not interested in masterpieces. He thought the public—and he didn't divide the public up into segments or strata of lowbrows, mediumbrows and high-brows—was able to appreciate and love good music.

But, generally, it was believed then that everyone competent to appreciate the best either went off to Europe for the summer music festivals, or withdrew to a vacation devoid of culture at one of the fashionable American resorts. Arnold, however, contended that the New Yorkers who remained in the city were just as able to enjoy good music as anyone else. Furthermore, he believed they were entitled to it.

He was delighted to discover that Commissioner Stover concurred. Stover was an idealist, a music-lover, a dreamer—but a constructive visionary.

Arnold and Franz Kaltenborn were engaged to conduct, on alternate weeks, eight weeks of orchestral concerts in the old pagoda bandstand in Central Park. Both conducted for four years. Arthur Farwell, the American composer, was appointed supervisor of the series. The first concert was given July 2, 1910.

One must stretch the imagination considerably to accept as credible my descriptions of those days. But remember, radio was still unknown, and the great nationwide offering of good music in huge outdoor summer concerts, in the further development of which Arnold later was to play such a vital part, had not even begun. This was the beginning—these orchestral concerts in Central Park, in 1910.

Sharp changes have taken place since then. For example, I wonder how many conductors of Arnold's ability today would conduct a concert and a rehearsal for a total of $25. How many musicians would be willing now to play for $7 a performance?

But what hunger the public had for good music! The success was immediate. Crowds of 10,000 to 30,000 would gather and, after each number, cheer and shout approval.

The bandstand was by no means as large or as acoustically adequate as the one now used by Edwin Franko Goldman. Nor was the seating and standing room as well arranged. The people crowded in and spilled out everywhere. When both afternoon and evening concerts were given on Saturdays and Sundays, many people would sit through both concerts. They would remain in their seats, many having brought food, while those without food were afraid to leave their seats for fear of losing them.

Some, however, had members of their families come to hold their places; others employed "sitters" while they hurried off for a bite to eat.

I have seen crowds sitting through the rain, begging that the program continue. Applause for encores would extend for minutes, accompanied by "bravos" and shouts and hats flying in the air. But if one dared talk during the playing, he was hissed.

Today, with great orchestras available at the turn of the knob, or in vast amphitheatres under the stars, the public can hardly be expected to comprehend the scarcity of, or the hunger for, good music in 1910.

Besides the memories of those days as musical history, there are so many recollections that are just personal. Arnold always wanted me to be at every performance and, of course, I wanted to be there. No seats were reserved. Every place was filled long before the concert began, at least an hour or more.

Our younger baby, Cecilia, still had to be taken about in a carriage. The Park Superintendent arranged for a small bench to be kept aside by the attendants. When I arrived, just a half-hour early, wheeling Cecilia, the bench would be carried down front for me and placed almost beside the bandstand. There I was assured of a good seat; and Cecilia, three, and Eleanor, seven, behaved like the angels they were.

But the sight of an empty bench, even a small one, being carried down the aisle for the use of a "privileged" person caused so many irate complaints that we had to discontinue this practice. The demand for seats was just too great even for the conductor to have family privileges.

One incident of these Central Park concerts became famous, not only in the annals of music, but of American humor. This is the way it happened. At one of the concerts, Arnold was conducting the Beethoven *"Lenore" Overture* No. 3. The first trumpet player, Borodkin, was to leave the bandstand as unobtrusively as possible and, for the first of the two required off-stage trumpet calls, take a position about a hundred feet to the rear of the stand. For the second call, he was to move in about fifty feet closer.

All went well as Borodkin slipped out quietly and was ready for his cue for the first call. It began beautifully. To the players in the stand and the audience out in front it sounded so fine, with all the good tone and all the traditional *accelerando* and *ritardando* Beethoven intended. The last few notes, however, went quite wild, as if Borodkin had gone entirely to pieces.

As Arnold continued with the orchestra and went on to the second cue, he looked far from pleased. Of course, we were all on pins and needles as to what the second call would sound like. It rang out delightfully, this time played perfectly all the way through.

When Borodkin returned to his seat in the orchestra, all his colleagues saw his red face—much redder even than it should have been, for all his false notes. At intermission time he went to Arnold with his explanation. He related that he had started playing the first call when a heavy hand clutched his shoulder sternly and an angry voice demanded:

"Hey, you! Whatcha tryin' to do? Can'tcha hear there's a concert goin' on? Tryin' to spoil it! Cut it out!"

Borodkin's eerie notes had come as he tried to escape the ponderous grip on his shoulder. After struggling through the rest of the call, he turned to discover the owner of the angry voice was a policeman. Borodkin had a stiff argument with him, while the orchestra played on to the second cue. He convinced him, at least for the moment, that what he had been doing was part of the performance. Furthermore, he explained, he had to do it once more fifty feet closer.

As soon as Borodkin finished the second call, the policeman escorted him back to the bandstand. Nor was he satisfied until Arnold, and practically the entire orchestra, assured him that Beethoven had wanted the first call to sound as if outside the theatre and the second as if at the theatre doors.

Finally mollified, the policeman remarked, "Well, if you say so, it's all right with me. But when I seen this guy standin' in the bushes gettin' ready to play his cornet, and just a few feet away a concert goin' on, I says to myself, 'One note out of that bird and I'll run him in.' "

The moral if any: if you plan to play that *"Lenore" Overture* at an outdoor concert, be sure to notify the police.

Some years later, at a luncheon of musicians, Borodkin got another laugh from the incident. A conductor told the story—except that he said it happened at one of *his* concerts, and in Europe. Borodkin created roaring laughter when he got up and protested the theft. Over the years, however, he grew accustomed to hearing many variations of his experience.

All during Commissioner Stover's regime, from 1910 to 1913, the Central Park concerts were a tremendous success. Then, with a political change, the concerts were abandoned. But before their demise, the newspapers had written such descriptions as I quote:

"Half a dozen big lawns were thrown open to accommodate 20,000 persons who crowded Central Park Mall yesterday afternoon to hear the first open-air concert given by the city this year.

"At three o'clock, an hour before the concert was to begin, every settee within hearing distance was occupied and the asphalt space about the bandstand was filled with a restless throng. The driveway over Terrace Bridge was lined with carriages and automobiles, and the Casino pergola was crowded with listeners."

Commissioner Stover stated: "This pavilion where the orchestra plays served its purpose well, and now that the attendance is so large and so many complaints are made that thou-

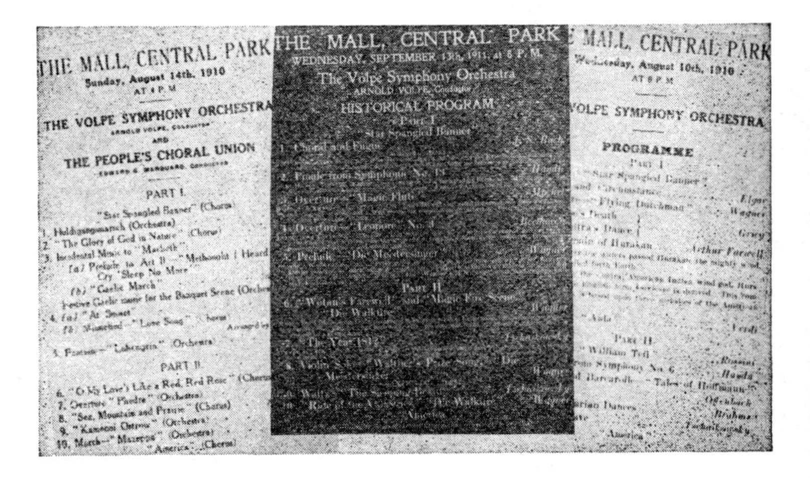
THE MALL, CENTRAL PARK
Sunday, August 14th, 1910

THE VOLPE SYMPHONY ORCHESTRA

AND

THE PEOPLE'S CHORAL UNION

PART I.

PART II.

6. "O My Love's Like a Red, Red Rose" (Chorus)

"America" (Chorus)

THE MALL, CENTRAL PARK
WEDNESDAY, SEPTEMBER 13th, 1911, at 8 P. M.

The Volpe Symphony Orchestra

HISTORICAL PROGRAM

THE MALL, CENTRAL PARK
Wednesday, August 10th, 1910

VOLPE SYMPHONY ORCHESTRA

PROGRAMME

Three Central Park Programs

sands cannot hear the music, I propose to have a funnel-shaped bandstand constructed with sounding apparatus for projecting the music to a great distance, as was so successfully done at Brighton and Manhattan beaches.

"It will enable everybody to hear the music distinctly as far back as the Casino."

One of the notable features that made Arnold's Central Park programs memorable to New Yorkers was that here, too, he gave many works of American composers. This he did at every feasible opportunity, in accord with his belief that musical development of America should include recognition of its own composers.

The magazine *Musical America* in an editorial said that municipal officials once "held the utilitarian notion that in order to retain paid positions it was necessary to regale the citizens with ragtime, turkey trots, and bunny hug compositions. Arnold Volpe changed all that, and to him the thanks of the community are due in rich measure."

This phrase, "Arnold Volpe changed all that," was deeply discerning. He was always supplanting old situations with new, always changing and bettering them. With the Young Men's Symphony Orchestra he had changed the outlook for young student musicians. With the Volpe Symphony Orchestra he had created opportunities for young professional musicians.

Even though the next city administration did not continue the Central Park concerts, the people of New York had demonstrated their appreciation for good music. It was only a matter of time before Arnold, again the pioneer, would be projecting greater things in music for the people.

But many other things were destined to take place before that would happen. There were such happy events, for instance, as the Shakespeare Festival by the Ben Greet Players, in Carnegie Hall. The Volpe Symphony Orchestra was selected to play a full incidental score for *As You Like It* and for *A Mid-summer Night's Dream.*

Then, in the series of popular Sunday evening concerts, inaugurated by R. E. Johnston in the Hippodrome at Sixth Avenue and Forty-third Street, many prominent soloists appeared with the Volpe Symphony Orchestra. Later this series was taken over and managed by Sol Hurok.

The years were crowded with new ventures, new triumphs and solid progress. Now, in looking back, I can see how they were building to much greater moments in our lives.

Chapter XI

EUROPE AND WORLD WAR I—1914

IN LOOKING OVER the score of a new symphony submitted with the hope that it would be given its American premiere by the Volpe Symphony Orchestra, Arnold was surprised to find it an exceptionally fine work.

When he made inquiries about the composer, Pietro Floridia, he heard an amazing story. Floridia's operas and other works had been given successfully in Italy—until someone started a malicious rumor that he had the evil eye!

The fantastic gossip forced him to leave Italy. He came to New York and was in desperate financial straits when Arnold looked him up. It was another opportunity of the kind to which Arnold's altruism and generosity always responded. It was instinctive with him. Floridia, the artist, and his artistry were in need of help.

When Arnold announced the symphony was to be given its American premiere in 1912, he was deluged with warnings. Something simply dreadful was bound to happen to his family, his home, or to Carnegie Hall. The thing that really did happen, however, was that Floridia, who was destitute because of this medieval persecution, accepted a paying engagement for the evening of the premiere and didn't hear his symphony performed or the ovation it received.

In appreciation for Arnold's kindness, Floridia, after hearing me sing, offered to give me daily lessons. He thought I had the making of a fine career. My husband and my daughters were primarily on my mind, and I, therefore, had given little attention to my voice.

Now that the girls were going to school, I could devote a few hours each day to it. I practiced diligently, much to the

Old bandstand at Central Park, 1910

Crowds attending Municipal Concerts at the Mall in Central Park, 1910-1913

AEOLIAN HALL

THURSDAY EVENING, JANUARY 15, 1914
AT EIGHT THIRTY O'CLOCK

MME. MARIE VOLPE

IN SONG RECITAL

THE friends of Mme. Marie Volpe, to whom she has been known through her active connection with the Volpe Symphony Society, will be glad to learn that she is about to make her appearance as a singer on the concert platform.

Gifted with a voice of exceptional quality, and endowed with rare aptitude for the art of song, it is, however, only on account of her remarkable progress, and the development of her vocal powers within the past two years under the tuition of Signor Pietro Floridia, that Mme. Volpe has been induced to enter upon a professional career.

Mme. Volpe has yet to complete her vocal training. It is hoped that the success of this, her first concert, will go far toward enabling her further to pursue her studies and to reach the high artistic standard which she has set for herself.

It is safe to predict that, under favorable conditions, Mme. Volpe is bound soon to become one of the leading exponents of the art of song.

ARNOLD VOLPE.

PROGRAMME

I.

a. "Se tu m'ami" .... ***Pergolesi***
b. Andenken }
c. "Ich liebe dich" } .... ***Beethoven***
d. "Voi che sapete" (Nozze di Figaro) . . ***Mozart***

II.

a. "De Himmel hat eine Thräne geweint" }
b. Frühlingsnacht } . . ***Schumann***
c. Der Wanderer .... ***Brahms***
d. Wanderer's Nachtlied }
e. Erlkönig } .... ***Schubert***

III.

a. Ein Traum }
b. "Gelb rollt mir zu Füssen" } . . ***Rubinstein***
c. "Glaub nicht dem schnellem Wort," ***Tschaikowsky***
d. Die Loreley .... ***Liszt***
e. Träume .... ***Wagner***

IV.

a. Traum durch die Dämmerung }
b. Zueignung } ***R. Strauss***
c. "Wenn mich wie eine Kalte Woge" . . . . ***Volpe***
d. Unter Sternen .... ***Weingartner***

SIGNOR PIETRO FLORIDIA AT THE PIANO

STEINWAY PIANO USED

(Marie Volpe)—My first concert

delight of Arnold, who, I suddenly discovered, had long been anxious for me to sing professionally. During the first ten years of our married life, he had said almost nothing about it. Now, when the time seemed ripe, he made an emphatic point of it.

For two years I worked hard under Floridia's instruction. He was a great musician, interpreter and composer. But I was not satisfied with his method for my voice. The lessons began to irritate me to the point that poor Arnold had to go with me to restrain me from losing my temper. I was not at all sure what was wrong and neither was Arnold.

We talked over all aspects of the situation. It involved other considerations beside my doubts about Floridia's methods as applied to me. With others, he seemed to be effective. Moreover, Floridia's studio was now crowded with pupils recommended by us. This had not only restored him to a good living, but also had enabled him to bring his wife and daughter from Switzerland. How could I leave his studio? If I went elsewhere for instruction, most of his pupils would follow.

Arnold thought it best for me to give a recital, then go to Europe for further study. He insisted that since I had helped launch him, it was now his turn to do the same for me. I was really stunned. I did not want a career. I wanted my home, my family, and to be at my husband's side to help him.

Suddenly to face all the intricacies of a professional career! It was foreign to my personal desires and ambitions. Nevertheless, I was learning more and more that when Arnold Volpe made up his mind to do something, or wanted something done, I might as well say "Amen" right away. Sooner or later I would have to give in.

To prove to me his judgment of my voice, he had me sing for some of the best musicians—Pasquale Amato, Mme. Margaret Matzenauer, Otto Goeritz and others. Even though they were friends and frequent guests at our house, I could not discount the integrity of their opinions. To my disappointment, they all agreed with Arnold that my voice was unusually good and well worth a sacrifice. After hearing me, Henry Krehbiel, music critic for the New York *Tribune,* arranged an audition with Mme. Marcella Sembrich.

A recital was arranged, and the press, too, sided with Arnold, saying my voice held generous promise, encouraging the plan for the European training.

So I was left with no more arguments. Arrangements were made for me to go to Paris to study under Professor Jean Bouhy, considered one of the best voice teachers in Europe. Somehow, it seemed, all this could still be prevented, and I hoped to forestall it —until at last we broke up our home, sold our household goods, and I was packed and ready for departure.

Arnold never learned of my inner struggles and what it meant to me to go through with it. Then a thought came to me. I would use the trip for the good of Arnold. I would act as his representative and try to get some engagements for him.

It was almost impossible in those days to be called to conduct a major orchestra in the United States without a European reputation, and I realized the lack of it was the only reason Arnold had not been invited.

His abilities as a conductor had been attested by his achievements time and time again. Music critics acclaimed him. The best musicians not only agreed with the critics, but went much further in recognizing his gifts as a conductor. But all these judgments and praises had been based on American accomplishments. The United States was still not sure enough of itself musically to accept talent that did not bear the European stamp.

I would arrange for that, I decided. It changed my entire attitude toward the trip. Arnold, without understanding why I had grown more excited, was delighted. With my head teeming with plans of what I would do for Arnold, I left with the two girls in March, 1914, for Paris. An older woman friend, who spoke French fluently, travelled with us. I put the girls in school in Neuilly, near Paris.

Professor Bouhy heard me sing and accepted me for daily lessons. He, too, predicted a brilliant career. He was a charming and attractive person.

As wife of a "chef d'orchestre," I had entrée to all musical events. Among others I recall, I attended every performance of the Boston Opera Company, which was giving a series with some of the greatest singers and conductors. I studied French, and, of course, worked hard with my voice.

Before long, I again realized I was not using my voice correctly. My throat began to bother me. After singing a short while, I would get hoarse. It discouraged me very much. The only answer I could draw from Professor Bouhy was "Je ne sais pas pourquoi."

Arnold, who was staying with my parents in New York until he finished his work of the season, was scheduled to arrive in June. Although we had been separated less than three months, it was a gay reunion. How wonderfully that summer of 1914 began. He was delighted to hear his daughters speaking French like natives. He laughed with me when I asked in French for apples and got potatoes or ordered dessert and was served kidney sauté.

Before starting our summer travels, we left the girls with a governess in a hotel at Pepinster, Belgium, not far from Professor Bouhy's summer villa, as he had suggested. Our first stop was at Loschwitz, near Dresden, where Professor Auer had invited us for the celebration of his seventieth birthday. He said he would arrange for us to hear some of his students, and one of his "wunderkinder." The boy played for Arnold for hours. The father asked us to call the following day, and the boy played again. Arnold was deeply impressed.

The father was eager to take his son to the United States. He begged me to manage an American tour for him. I replied that I was not interested in promoting the career of anyone except Arnold Volpe, and told Herr Heifetz I could not undertake the management of his boy Jascha.

In Berlin, where I had lived as a youngster, Arnold and I enjoyed a round of sightseeing to all the beloved places I remembered—where I had lived, where I had gone to school, where I had skipped rope—all so much more delightful with my husband by my side.

We called on Arthur M. Abel, the Berlin correspondent for the *Musical Courier*. He arranged an audition for me with Mr. and Mrs. Emmerich, who were the first to diagnose my voice correctly. Everyone previously had insisted I was a dramatic soprano and forced me to sing in the high registers. This was the main reason for my throat trouble. Mr. Emmerich called my voice a "jugendliches" soprano, which might develop into a dramatic soprano. Personally I considered myself a mezzo-soprano and preferred everything written in the rich middle register. We made arrangements for me to study the following winter with the Emmerichs and found for the girls a delightful Waldschule outside of Berlin.

Then, through Mr. Abel, we met some of the foremost concert managers. Arnold was engaged to conduct the Berlin Philharmonic. Negotiations were started and were well under way for other engagements in London, Vienna and Paris. Everything for the coming year seemed to be working out on schedule.

We had coffee with Josef and Rosina Lhevinne in their new home in Wannensee, and with the Coenraad Boses, and left for Karlsbad. The day we arrived World War I broke out. In a few hours the place was almost deserted of civilians. It was frightening to watch the first mobilization trains packed with soldiers. I asked some of the high Austrian officials whether our children were safe in Belgium. They answered, "The safest place in the world."

We had tea with Josef Stransky and other musicians. They did not seem to be much disturbed. However, I began to worry.

I sensed the seriousness of affairs and wanted to get to my children.

Arnold had made plans for us to visit many people in many places and begged me at least to keep the appointment with Ossip Gabrilowitsch's family. He so wanted me to know Gabrilowitsch's parents and his sister Pauline and them to know me. They were spending the summer in Wiesbaden. We arrived there in the morning.

The air was filled with rumors. One was that the Germans were marching toward Luxembourg, which was not far from our children. Right after luncheon with the Gabrilowitsches, we hurried to the railroad station. Pauline Gabrilowitsch took us there, so kind in her efforts to calm us. We heard the tramp of marching feet all about. It took us years to forget that sound.

After three hours of terrifying confusion, we were told that all trains leaving Wiesbaden for Belgium were being given orders not to stop before Brussels. We almost lost our minds. We begged and implored every official to have our train stop at Herbesthal, near Pepinster. Finally, one of the officials (he must have been a father) promised to have the train halt for us.

Rushing to the hotel, we found our daughters alone. The young governess had already fled to her family. Our train had been absolutely the last into Belgium. After that, it would have been impossible for us to have reached our children until after the war.

But when we were reunited, nothing else mattered. Somehow we reached London. As we registered with the American Citizens Committee in London, we were relieved to discover that our passports were all in good order, and we had few of the troubles so many others experienced.

Before I left for Europe, in March of 1914, I was advised by friends not to travel with two minor children without a passport. So I asked Arnold to be sure to carry his citizenship papers when he left the United States to meet us. This precaution proved wise, as well as a great comfort and security to us. Those who did not have passports waited for days and weeks at the American Consulates and Embassies.

Meanwhile, although we didn't know it at the time, our friends in New York were apprised of our safety. We found out later that the *Sun* on August 13th said:

"The first list of Americans who have registered with the Citizens Committee in London, and who are being sent home as rapidly as boat passage can be secured for them, is concluded this morning.

"Among the best-known names in this morning's list are Brandon Tynan, the actor, whose last conspicuous role was Joseph in 'Joseph and His Brethren'; G. Creighton Webb, major in the Rough Riders, ex-attaché of the American Embassy at Paris and brother of S. Seward Webb; and Arnold Volpe, whose concerts are features of New York's winter music. Mrs. Volpe is with her husband."

Oh, if the writer of that last short sentence I have quoted could have understood the true meaning of it. We were together.

After a tense wait of three weeks, we finally got passage for home. As the murky shores of Europe faded astern, thought rose numbly: "And so here we go home—without a European reputation for Arnold." But that didn't seem to matter as we headed for America. Arnold, after all, had found his real challenge in America. He was equal to it without any further help from Europe. He was an American, and for that I silently thanked God.

We were again thanking God for that a few days later as we approached the Statue of Liberty and, with everyone else on the ship, knelt down on the deck on our knees and sang our American national anthem.

Chapter XII

VOLPE INSTITUTE 1916-1920

OUR HOME always had been the rendezvous of musicians and patrons of music. Often they came in response to invitations, and there was a great deal of delightful "dropping in." We loved it.

Two years of struggle, disappointment and readjustment followed our return from Europe. I had expected to stay abroad at least three years, and therefore we had broken up our home and sold all our household goods in order to have enough money for our expenses. It all seems so foolish and impractical now; but I remember that Arnold's wish and his ambition for me prompted us to take this fateful journey.

We found it difficult to find ourselves again, although Arnold kept busy with his various activities—the Young Men's Symphony Orchestra, the Brooklyn Institute Orchestra, and his violin class. My parents, who had a large apartment at 480 Central Park West, invited us to live with them until we could work out our problems. We stayed with them until the summer of 1916, when we were able once more to furnish a home of our own.

The extent of our providing a gathering place depended in large part on the size of the apartment or house we had at the time. One four-year period was especially rich and lively in its blend of musical and social life.

It began when Arnold established the Volpe Institute of Music in the fall of 1916, war conditions having made it impossible to continue the Volpe Symphony Orchestra after we returned from Europe in 1914. The Institute was an outgrowth of his success as a violin teacher. His name now in New York educational and musical circles carried a reputation that made him the logical one to head such a school.

The faculty roster comprised about twenty. Besides Arnold, who took charge of the violin and ensemble classes, there were four other figures of eminence. In looking over the original announcement of the Institute, I notice that their names and achievements were considered so well known that it did not bother to say what each was going to teach. It was simply assumed everybody in New York would know. The assumption was safe, for the distinguished men were: David Bispham, concert and opera singer, voice; Edwin Hughes, piano; Leon Rothier, Metropolitan Opera basso, voice; and Arkady Bourstin, violin.

We rented a four-story house at 146 West Seventy-seventh Street, in an accessible and fashionable section of the upper West Side. Our home was in the same house. It was a delightful arrangement, thoughtfully planned to suit Arnold's notions and mine. Both of us arranged our home life, our professional work and our social life, so that in some respects it was difficult to tell where one stopped and the other began. Our associations with musicians and patrons of music so filled our lives with rich satisfactions that we found little reason to seek many acquaintances or interests outside.

Each day, musicians and others who in one way or another were deeply interested in music enlivened our home with their comings and goings from morning until night. In addition to this fairly constant flow of like-minded people, there were special occasions, some of them formal events.

At frequent intervals, for example, the Institute would hold recitals. Basically, they were performances by outstanding students. But members of the faculty would also perform, and renowned artists would play as guests of honor—Eugene Ysaye, Ossip Gabrilowitsch, members of the Flonzaley Quartet, Mischa Elman and many others of equal distinction.

They were there for a combination of reasons. First, they were all our dear personal friends. They were also Arnold's intellectual colleagues, laboring in the same cultural ways as we to bring joy to others; beyond and above all else, they were our spiritual companions. This beautiful kind of friendship, compounded of many elements, is not easy for me to describe. I am sure, though, it will be clear to those who love music, for even if, like myself, they lack exact words, through glorious experience they will know what I mean. Arnold and I found so much of our happiness in such a blissful meeting of minds, such complete understanding of spirit, and in wonderful working together.

The Institute almost immediately won a very high place in the musical life of New York and, as one writer for the press said, "had taken its place at one bound in the very forefront of musical schools in the metropolis."

It was our great pleasure to devote one of our receptions at the Institute to introducing Professor Leopold Auer. He and Mme. Bogutska-Stein arrived from Europe in 1918. Arnold had been his first pupil to settle in New York, and over the years Professor Auer and Arnold had kept in close touch.

We had last seen him at Loschwitz in the gay and lovely early summer of 1914, when we were still oblivious of the cataclysm that was to descend in a few weeks. Auer was Austrian by birth, and although for a long, long time he had been a citizen of Russia, such matters of original nationality had to be taken into consideration in the 1918 atmosphere.

Any trepidations we had about the success of our reception for Auer, the artist, were immediately dispelled. The only confusion resulted from the almost simultaneous arrival of the approximately four hundred guests. The receiving line extended out on the sidewalk for much too long a time for the comfort of any hostess. Even though the guests were what one of the newsmen with an aptitude for terse phrases called "the blue book of New York musical life," they were patient, and their graciousness soon restored my poise.

The rooms of our home and of the Institute that day were filled with an aura I shall never forget. Arnold was sublimely pleased to be able to pay his tribute to the one responsible for his musical education. Professor Auer was witty and delightful in his reminiscences of Arnold at the Imperial Conservatory, telling many incidents of Arnold's prowess as a gifted student. He dwelt admiringly on Arnold's fortitude when, so poignantly anxious to gain admission, he had stood in the cold on the steps, waiting for Auer each morning.

The reception would have been successful anywhere, but there at the Volpe Institute, where Arnold was handing on his knowledge to another generation of musicians, the event assumed a heartier significance that infused the whole gathering.

The Institute continued with high success for several years; then, a circumstance that had nothing to do with its educational values closed it. The year 1920 may be remembered by some as the year the Nineteenth Amendment made woman's suffrage effective, or the year Sacco and Vanzetti were alleged to have shot the paymaster. But to me it was the terrible year of the post-war housing shortage.

We held only a lease on the house on Seventy-seventh Street, subject to sale of the property. It was sold, and we had only sixty days to vacate the Institute. Our frantic search for an adequate house or apartment was futile. We had to discontinue the school, break up our home and move into a hotel. It was awful. Arnold always wanted his studio right where he lived. In a hotel this was impossible, and he was most unhappy. But it was only for a short time, for in a year we again were in a place of our own.

Chapter XIII

GABRILOWITSCH FRIENDSHIP

IT WAS USUALLY "Volpe" and "Gabrilowitsch" between them. Rarely did they use first names with each other. In those days everything was more formal than now. They were days of dignity with every one, and Arnold Volpe and Ossip Gabrilowitsch had behind them the traditions of those earlier and even more formal days at the Imperial Conservatory in St. Petersburg.

I have told of the beginning of their friendship at the Conservatory—with the stiff official patronage of the Czar, whose idea of "dropping around of a morning" was to stalk in with full cortege in burnished regalia and pulverize even the aplomb of Director Anton Rubinstein.

At the Conservatory, faculty and pupils maintained all the formal customs of salutation. Students never dreamed of calling their professors the Russian equivalent of "prof." They never even thought of them with such informality. In addressing each other, they were equally respectful. Virtually every student was looking forward to the time when he, too, would be a figure in the musical world, and each viewed the other as a future personage. In this spirit of old-school comradeship, Arnold and Ossip Gabrilowitsch often called each other "Celebrated" and "Eminent," especially in letters.

Of course, when I heard them do that in New York, it was after they had truly achieved the right to such complimentary titles, and somehow these terms, in light of the fact, seemed to hold an odd bit of humor. Today, it might seem a bit strange to hear old friends addressing each other so formally, but it never did then.

In the bond between Arnold and Gabrilowitsch, there was more than a tie as individuals. Mingled with it was the great admiration held for the whole Gabrilowitsch family, especially the parents and Ossip's sister, Pauline Gabrilowitsch. I have as a keepsake of that great friendship the simple, graceful little bronze figure of a dachshund given to Arnold in Russia so long ago by Pauline. Year by year its meaning became greater, just as the Gabrilowitsch friendship grew older and deeper.

Gabrilowitsch made his first American appearance in 1900. He was greeted with enthusiasm, and thereafter, whether in Europe or America, his name ranked with the highest. His piano style revealed delicacy and restraint—yet possessed brilliant power. How Arnold and I admired his depth of expression! "The poet of the piano," as he was so often called, was an appropriate description.

When Gabrilowitsch was only about fourteen years old, you will recall, he played the accompaniment for Arnold's violin solos before the board of examination at the Imperial Conservatory.

As far as I can remember, Gabrilowitsch always had some trouble with his digestion. I never forgot about it when he came to dine with us. There would usually be for him some white meat of chicken, some toast, milk, a custard and a baked apple. He was so appreciative of any little attention to him.

He first saw our baby, Eleanor, when she was six weeks old. He turned to us and in German gave her that touching little European term of sweet endearment, "Meine Kleine Braut"—my little bride, which he always continued to call her.

For one with such vast power at the piano, with such astounding range of expression, his voice was in surprising contrast. It was *always* gentle, always *pianissimo.* Yet, he could speak so warmly with it, almost make it glow.

He always wore high collars, right up to the firm line of his cheek, and I noticed how little difference there was between the white linen and the paleness of his skin. I noticed it the more, perhaps, because no matter how excited he might be over some idea he was discussing with Arnold, the color of his cheeks never changed, whereas Arnold's ruddy visage at such times picked up an extra glow.

They were equally ebullient about new ventures, and it seemed they could never get together without hatching one. Although their enthusiastic scheming did not always lead to momentous sequels, it frequently did. One occasion came when Arnold included Gabrilowitsch's *Rhapsodie, Op. 6,* in a program of the Volpe Symphony Orchestra in March, 1907.

Arnold asked him to conduct it. Until then, Gabrilowitsch's career had included only composing and performing. He had never conducted, and he demurred. Under Arnold's insistence, however, he did and conducted the *Rhapsodie* well. Gabrilowitsch got such a thrill doing it that after numerous analytical conferences with Arnold and considering it all carefully, he went off to Europe to study conducting under Weingartner and others. Thus began the groundwork for his conductorship of the Detroit Symphony Orchestra which came to him twelve years later.

As I look at the time-stained letter Arnold received soon after that concert in 1907, I wonder if Gabrilowitsch ever concerned himself further with his thought about the genesis of conductors. He wrote:

"I sail for Europe tomorrow and before doing so I want to tell you once more how I enjoyed playing with your orchestra and what a pleasant thing it was for me to see *you* conduct. I have always known you to be a fine musician, but now I am absolutely convinced that the great work of your life is in that particular line.

"Conductors are born, not made. And you certainly are a born conductor. I could tell that easily after the first few bars I heard the orchestra play under your direction. And the more I listened, the more I was impressed by the truly remarkable way in which you forced your men to follow your artistic intentions.

"You have the authority, the repose and the solid good musicianship which are essential for a leader, and when I think that with a body of young and inexperienced musicians you accomplished such wonderful results, I feel sure that with a real first-class orchestra you will accomplish things that will be *great*.

"I wish you and your orchestra a splendid career and I certainly have no doubt that your future as a conductor will be a fine and brilliant one."

Whether Gabrilowitsch himself was "born" or "made," he became an excellent conductor, although the musical world always preferred to recognize him first for his performance at the piano.

Usually, a few weeks before Gabrilowitsch was scheduled to appear in New York, a brief, crisp letter would precede him. His letters were hardly ever like himself, being straightly worded, to the point and in tone almost distant. For example, late in March, 1918 he wrote Arnold:

"I am going to give three orchestral concerts in New York in April and May—the dates are April 18th, April 25th and May 2nd. I will appear as conductor and soloist, playing a concerto on each program. Will you conduct the concertos for me; and will you engage the orchestra, the same as you did last year?"

He would arrive a few days after the letter—so different himself. He and Arnold would have a wonderful time going over the list of orchestra men needed, and with amazing efficiency, interspersed with a great many pleasantries, would complete arrangements. Then they would settle down for a grand talk about what they had been doing since last they had seen each other.

Then, there would be the concerts and the reviews by the critics, and off Gabrilowitsch would go on his further round of appearances over the country. Soon after, there would come another flatly worded, typed letter:

"Now that our concert is over, let me thank you again for the splendid assistance you have given me in every way, both as a conductor and as a friend. Had it not been for your personal interest in the matter, I never could have secured such an excellent orchestra, and I want you to know that I do sincerely appreciate your support."

Gabrilowitsch, upon reading the typed letter before signing it, would realize how much it lacked the warmth he was trying to express. Down at the bottom in his own hand he would add, "You are a bully fellow!"

The morning after the last of these three Carnegie Hall concerts, there was a ring at our door. A man peering around a huge box held in his arms said he was from Tiffany's. I told him he must have the wrong house; we did not buy anything there. He insisted it was addressed to Arnold Volpe. We opened it, still thinking it was a mistake, until we found Ossip Gabrilowitsch's card saying it was a little expression of appreciation. The glorious clock of white marble embellished with gold and with two golden candelabra now have a place of honor in our daughter Eleanor's lovely Rochester home.

When Gabrilowitsch and Clara Clemens, the daughter of Mark Twain, were married, we were delighted. She was a contralto, and she and Gabrilowitsch often appeared in joint recitals. She took her singing lessons very seriously, and she encouraged me to sing.

I was still not interested in a career, but she insisted I should go on, and we always had a great deal to talk over about singing teachers and singing methods. Once, I recall, when we were having a conversation of this nature, Gabrilowitsch turned to Arnold, laughing, and exclaimed: "Good heavens, if we instrumentalists changed, or even considered changing, methods as often as singers, where, I ask you, would we be!" This caused them to go into a long interval of chuckling at our expense—at which we singers raised our eyebrows disdainfully, although we couldn't help agreeing that they had a point.

When Gabrilowitsch received the offer of the conductorship of the Detroit Symphony Orchestra and was considering it, he asked Arnold to go with him as associate conductor. I knew he was most hopeful, and I believe he assumed Arnold would go. For months, Arnold's studio was headquarters for the Detroit Symphony Orchestra, at which all the auditions for musicians were held. In the preparation, Gabrilowitsch leaned heavily on Arnold's experience as a conductor.

I think the only unhappy meal we ever had together was the luncheon at which Arnold was to give his decision to Gabrilowitsch. Gabrilowitsch seemed to foresee the answer even as we sat down. The atmosphere was tense and unlike any time we had ever been together. It was simply not in keeping with Arnold's career then to leave New York, so he declined. Gabrilowitsch was terribly disappointed, and would have blamed the decision on me, had I not sensed his deep feeling—almost chagrin—and at once declared the truth. It was Arnold's decision, and I had not influenced him.

It made no difference in our personal friendship. One of the delightful recollections is of Chicago, when we were there in 1925. Gabrilowitsch was scheduled to give an afternoon concert. Well in advance, we received a telegram to save both the afternoon and evening. When he arrived, we discovered that since his wife had so enjoyed and recommended *Blossom Time,* he had reserved three tickets, so we could go with him.

We had already seen it. But we did not say so, nor did Arnold tell him that he had not enjoyed it very much. I sat between the two of them. When the play had been going on a little while, Gabrilowitsch started a whispered, but violently heated, conversation in Russian. They just couldn't contain themselves. I couldn't understand their words, but there was no misunderstanding their attitude. Before the end of the second act, Gabrilowitsch asked if I would mind if we left.

Then we admitted we had seen it. Outside, where Gabrilowitsch and Arnold could really open up, they were most

Leopold Auer and Arnold Volpe taken at Loschwitz in 1914 on Professor Auer's 70th birthday

"To dear Arnold in deepest affection."—P. and Ossip Gabrilowitsch

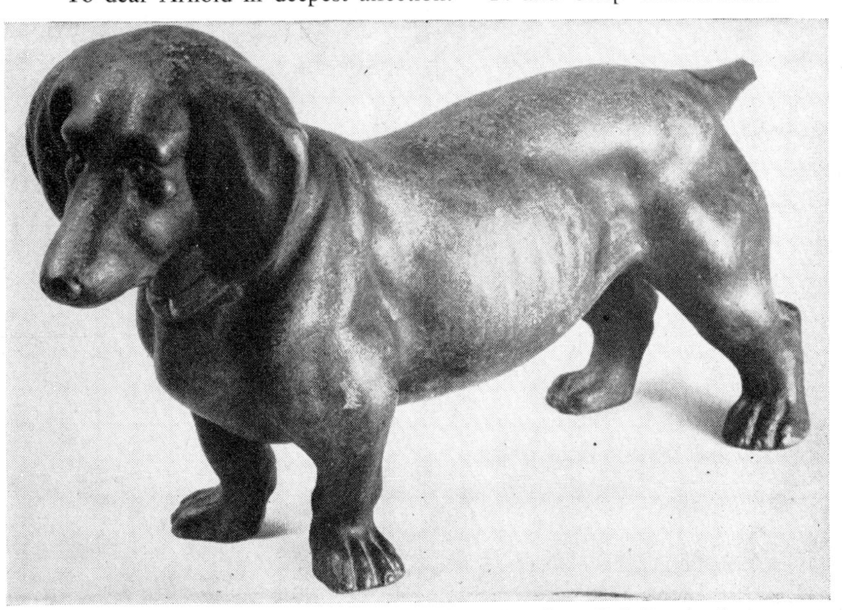

Bronze figurine given to Arnold by Pauline Gabrilowitsch

critical of having the wonderful music of Schubert presented that way.

We went to our apartment. There we had another one of those memorable evenings, sitting in a darkened room listening to Gabrilowitsch play, pouring forth his magnificent eloquence.

A letter Gabrilowitsch wrote about Arnold is one of my most treasured memorabilia. It is an unusual letter. Many cultured Russians learn to speak and write English perfectly. Yet, somehow, perhaps because it is the nature of musical minds, they are rarely as fluent with the pen as with their instruments. In this letter, which was written in response to a request for an appraisal of Arnold for an important post, Gabrilowitsch lacked neither conciseness nor a quality of emotion. He wrote:

"I am glad to tell you what I think of Mr. Volpe's musicianship. I can only speak of him in the very highest terms. I have known him for more than 25 years—in fact, ever since the days when I was a pupil of the Conservatory at St. Petersburg.

"He is a man of fine character, and in general musical equipment I think he is one of the finest men in this country and I can think of no one better suited to be at the head of an important musical organization.

"If my advice were asked, I would say, Take him as quickly as you can get him, for this is a chance that does not come often."

Through the years since their student days together at the Conservatory in St. Petersburg, Arnold and the Gabrilowitsch family always kept in touch with each other through correspondence. The following early letters, translated from the Russian, attest their devotion:

Copenhagen,
27 March 1898

My dearest Volpe:

You are no doubt very angry with me and you are right; I behaved toward you as swine. . . . Your letter received in good time. Your short letter I also received and until now could not collect my thoughts to answer. You will forgive me: but I have been travelling all the time and it was entirely impossible for me to write a lengthy letter. . . .

Your letter with a description of your trips and first steps in Johannesburg rejoiced me extraordinarily and excited my interest.

Now I will tell you a few words about myself. After we separated I gave in London one more concert and even attended the jubilee celebration of the Queen and then I left for St. Petersburg. In the autumn I again played in Berlin (with Nikisch), in Dresden, Frankfurt, London (Crystal Palace), Coln, Petersburg, Moscow, Stockholm and Copenhagen. In Petersburg and Moscow I had a great success, and in Moscow it was even a wild success: they carried me in the air and almost maimed me out of sheer rapture. I was invited by Count L. N. Tolstoy and played for him many times. On the whole, I played in Moscow 4 times and in Petersburg 3 times. Safonoff directed the Symphony.

One of the most pleasant concerts of the season was the Berlin Philharmonic, first because the Berlin public likes me very much and secondly to play with Nikisch is a real inspiration. At present I find myself in Copenhagen, where my success is so great that today I give here my fifth concert. At one of my concerts were present the Danish King and Queen, besides I played in the Palace of the Queen in the presence of the Empress Maria Feodorovna. From here I will go back to London, where I play in the Philharmonic and once more at the Crystal Palace.

How are you getting along . . . and how are your composing and directing affairs? Did your tour, about which you wrote me, materialize?

Am now finishing in London my musical season and am planning to spend the summer with my folks somewhere near Petersburg. Please write me at the old address: Troitzkaya 38, St. Petersburg and do write without fail.

Am sending this letter via Petersburg, since sister wants to add her regards. We often think of you, especially I.

Your old devoted friend
Ossip Gabrilowitsch

St. Petersburg
31 March, '98

Dear Arkádee Lvovitch:

Am sending you hereby my heartiest greetings and best wishes. You write us so seldom and we are so interested in your Leben und Treiben. I can imagine how you must have become by now a real Englishman, right?

Please write about yourself, don't be lazy, we'll answer you likewise. You know everything about Ossip from his letter, and therefore will say nothing about him.

Cordially yours,
N. Gabrilowitsch

St. Petersburg,
September 15, 1900
Kabinetzkaya St.
House 9.

Dear Friend Volpe:

You are not right if you are angry with me. All my fault is that I did not answer your very dear letter from Johannesburg, immediately. It is true many months have lapsed before I had answered your letter. I wrote together with my sister and sent the letter registered to the address P.O. Box 2830, Johannesburg.

During this past year I didn't receive any news from you, and so one very lovely day, I wrote you a letter which I had sent to Joanas, in London, but I noticed that you did not receive this letter, either. So, I can see that fate doesn't allow us to correspond.

Should you think that I had forgotten you or became cold to you—You are greatly mistaken—for how can it be!

No!

Ossip G.

"I shall remember you forever!"

You can see how you are in my memory, not only you but also your creations and even the text of your Romances.

"I still remember"

"And also"

"And many others"

St. Petersburg
30 March, 1901

Dear Arkádee Lvovitch!

Thousand thanks for your good letter. You cannot imagine the pleasure that it gave us. How many times did we reread it and how many times was it read in the circle of our dearest friends. Everybody thought of you. Ah, if one could receive more often such interesting letters. Your letter was written in such an expressive and artistic style that no one could write in a more literary way and you say that you forgot your Russian language!!

Are your relatives still in Johannesburg? . . . Did you receive the musical calendar that I sent for you? Did you have a chance to dance with Wright?? . . .

I hope that you will not let us wait much longer with your answer. We will be pleased to hear from you soon.

Friendly regards,
P. Gabrilowitsch

P. S. Ossip sends greetings, likewise my mother.

When we last saw Gabrilowitsch he was very ill. We motored to Detroit in the hope of seeing him in time. Fortunately, when we arrived it was one of his "better days"; he was dressed and sitting in his garden with his dear Clara. Greeting us most affectionately, he put his arms around my husband and said, "Arnold, you are a fine man."

They talked about Arnold's work. Gabrilowitsch offered to send some orchestral works and even talked of coming to play with Arnold's orchestra the following winter. In the Russian fashion, he kissed us both as we said good-bye. As we left the garden, he waved. We could see in that effort how terribly weak he was, but there was real hope in our hearts that he would recover. It was a harsh shock, only a month later, when he passed away.

The little bronze dog Arnold so treasured is a durable momento of that great friendship. It brings back memories of that day in the summer of 1914 when Arnold and I visited the Gabrilowitschs in Wiesbaden, and the lovely Pauline took us to the railroad station; of the elder Gabrilowitschs, whose gracious home life meant so much to Arnold as a student at the Conservatory; of the friendly letters exchanged over the years between Arnold and Pauline; of the concerts, with Gabrilowitsch at the piano and Arnold with the baton for the orchestral accompaniment of the concertos; of the wan face of Gabrilowitsch that day in his garden and the sad, worried look of Clara; of the way Arnold and Gabrilowitsch, in the old-school way, used to address each other as "Celebrated" and "Eminent."

Chapter XIV
STADIUM CONCERTS — *The Vision*

A YEAR AGO (1949), the loudspeakers in Berlin, where I spent my girlhood, were telling about Arnold Volpe. The radio story was in German. It was broadcast by the Voice of America in the series beamed to Europeans by the United States Government, interpreting America to peoples abroad.

Why did our Government think this story important to listeners in other lands? Because the programs are about major achievements in America. This one told how Arnold pioneered the Stadium Concerts in New York. Here are extracts from a translation of the broadcast:

"When, in June, 1918, under the direction of the beloved Arnold Volpe, the first series of concerts began, there were many music lovers in New York who were most skeptical and predicted the idea of high-class summer concerts would be a fiasco.

"Some agreed it would be possible to succeed with waltzes and light music, but when it came to the *Pathetique* or the *Eroica*—that would be just impossible.

"Volpe would not allow himself to be discouraged. The series, which was to be tried out for two weeks, began June 23, 1918; when fourteen days had passed, even the greatest skeptics had to admit they were wrong. Night after night the Lewisohn Stadium was filled to the last seat, and Volpe decided to extend his first season for another five weeks. The following year, 1919, was planned for eight weeks. This was the beginning."

The broadcaster went on to say:

". . . As I have repeatedly mentioned the name of the Lewisohn Stadium, some listeners may be under the false impression that at the time of the erection of the Stadium, the idea of concerts was included. This is not so. The Lewisohn Stadium is the gift of a New York philanthropist to the youth of New York. It is located close to the City College, and during the spring, autumn and winter is used for athletic programs.

"When Arnold Volpe looked about for a place to give classical music, he contacted the City College administration, and thus it came to pass that for two summer months, June 15th to the middle of August, the Lewisohn Stadium belongs to the young and old, to all who love music and wish to listen to good music.

"When one speaks about the concerts, one cannot forget to mention the name of the woman who, since the beginning with Arnold Volpe, in 1918, has indefatigably worked for the organization and its continuance, and who even today holds the reins with the same enthusiasm. Whenever money is needed, Mrs. Charles S. Guggenheimer is there to raise it. It is understandable, with tickets from 30 cents to $1.80, that this is a deficit enterprise. Mrs. Guggenheimer sees to it that the supply is there.

". . . These concerts have become the model for other musical organizations over the entire United States. A summer music season, such as the Lewisohn Stadium Concerts in New York, can now be found in every region—from the Great Lakes to Texas. The famous Hollywood Bowl, the Ravinia festivals in Chicago, the Robin Hood Dell concerts of the Philadelphia orchestra, the Watergate concerts of the Washington Symphony orchestra, and many other summer concerts, are the direct result of the success which Arnold Volpe had in 1918 with his first concert at the Lewisohn Stadium."

This overseas broadcast, skillfully written by Egon Stadelman, echoes other notable critiques of the Stadium, for example, that delightfully written history by Olin Downes, music critic of the New York *Times,* whose paper devoted a half page of its Sunday section to a piece on the 25th anniversary of the Stadium performances (1943). He wrote:

"On June 23, 1918, when Arnold Volpe raised his baton for the audience to join with the orchestra in the performance of *The Star-Spangled Banner,* the Stadium Concerts were an embryonic and local affair, packed with possibilities for the future, but still for the time being a local issue. This was partly due to the fact that at that time the radio had not yet become an instrument in common use for national, let alone international, communication. . . .

"Now, thanks to radio for one thing and the impressive artistic development for another, the Stadium Concerts have national as well as local significance. . . .

"In a 25 year cycle we have as a people learned many things in relation both to each other and to art itself. One of the heartening signs of this growth is the fact that . . . there will be no ban upon music by composers of Axis nations. In 1918, it was necessary to forbid performance of either German or Austrian compositions. . . .

"It would be hard to praise too highly, in retrospect, the faith and energy of those who believed in the Stadium idea. Arnold Volpe conceived it.

"Its realization was made possible by Adolph Lewisohn . . . and by Mrs. Charles Guggenheimer and a group of associates who made Volpe's dream a reality. Twenty-five years ago it was looked upon as something in the nature of a noble experiment. Volpe, when he outlined his plan to the committee who backed him, was certain of its value. Others were not.

"It was the general belief that in the summertime audiences would prefer 'light' to 'serious' music, especially of the symphonic variety. The daily toiler, white-collared or otherwise, would not care during the warm evening to sit and listen to music which needed 'knowledge' and 'concentration' for its real understanding. 'Pop' concerts, beer-garden programs and the like were of proved efficacy. But Bach, Brahms, Debussy, Sibelius were something else again, and not for general audiences or for people who had not before been exposed to symphonic music."

Mr. Downes was quite correct in this appraisal, written at the quarter-century mark of the Stadium. Indeed, the growth of the idea of the concerts to national significance had been remarked in 1936 by Howard Taubman, also of the *Times* Music Staff, while the concerts were yet in their teens. I quote from his article in *Today,* as condensed in the *Readers Digest*:

"Only two decades ago the musical life of the nation went soundly asleep from May to October. There were no summer operas, orchestras, or solo recitals, and no radio. Desperate music lovers could only make music themselves, play their phonographs, or go to Europe for the festivals.

"In the summer of 1918 Arnold Volpe started an experiment in New York. Together with a group of musicians drawn from the city's various orchestras, a chorus and several soloists, he gave a series of concerts in the Lewisohn Stadium, the football field of the College of the City of New York. Instead of failure, as was freely predicted, the series was an immense success. . . . The programs were not gay waltzes or stirring marches, but masterpieces. . . .

"How a good idea travels in these United States! The pioneer Lewisohn Stadium series, still in its teens, has achieved the repute of a national institution. And what a picture its companions would make if we could see them all at once."

Many other earlier and later résumés of Arnold's connection with the Stadium Concerts pile on the kudos until one can almost hear the thesauri rustling in the energetic search for superlatives. But all these excellently written pieces of journalism and literature leave out so much. Perhaps the time has come now to tell it as I knew it.

It was not altogether as pretty a story as it looked to those who viewed it from the outside. I think I should tell how

Arnold's artistic rights in the great pioneering venture were sold out behind his back for as little as $10,000. All was not sweetness and light. In the beginning there was much uphill work.

As a prelude, one spring day in 1917, Louis Fehr, the able publicity man for the New York City Park Department, came to Arnold.

Adolph Lewisohn had given the Stadium to the college that year for athletic purposes. Mr. Fehr asked Arnold if he would conduct six band concerts there. He did and they were successful. The stadium was crowded, for the seats were free; the City paid the costs. Musicians received $5 a concert and $2 for a rehearsal; the soloist got $8 and Arnold received $10 for a rehearsal and $15 for conducting a concert.

Arnold looked over the Stadium carefully. He had long been convinced that the musical tastes of the people were far beyond band concerts. This fact, plus the facilities of the huge stadium, he felt, added to something more than the Park Department's meager grasp of possibilities.

We talked it over together, at great length, working out the myriad details, checking every artistic and business aspect. We felt that with economical management, even at very low prices for seats, symphonic concerts could be given on a nearly self-supporting if not completely self-supporting basis.

We finally distilled the whole project to its essence. Arnold and I carefully kept documents, letters, etc., so I quote from the first announcement:

"The plan is to give high-class, open-air concerts at the City College Stadium nightly for ten weeks at popular prices—10, 25 and 50 cents.

"A fundamental feature of the plan is free admission to soldiers and sailors in uniform.

"In these times of stress it is of the greatest importance to provide healthy amusements for the masses. The value of music in stimulating patriotism is generally recognized."

The season's length was revised to seven weeks, with still a total of fifty concerts, and it was decided that the fifty programs would be given without a single composition of Wagner, Beethoven, Brahms, or any other German or Austrian composer. This restriction, of course, was not an aesthetic one, but simply in line with the general patriotic thinking of the time.

Arnold and I considered several plans for carrying out the over-all project. The first, which appealed to us both very much, was to affiliate ourselves with Julius Hopp, who had conceived the idea of introducing low-cost tickets to musical events for students and workers. He was most enthusiastic over our idea. It might have worked out better had we gone ahead with him. But we decided on another procedure.

Meanwhile, in the spring of 1918, I called Dr. Thomas A. Storey, who, as director of hygiene buildings and laboratories, administered the use of Mr. Lewisohn's athletic gift. He gave me an option on the stadium, providing time enough to work out the financial details—if we hurried.

May 16, 1918

Mrs. Arnold Volpe,
146 West 77th Street,
New York City, N. Y.

My dear Mrs. Volpe:

I am authorized to advise you that the Stadium and Field are now being reserved tentatively for your project from June 15th, 1918 to September 1st, 1918, with the understanding that your use of this property for the purposes for which you have in view will depend upon the execution of a written agreement mutually satisfactory to the College and to you, on or before June 1st, 1918.

If you will indicate to me your legal representative, I will send him shortly an agreement form for his consideration.

Very truly yours,
Thomas A. Storey
Director Hygiene Buildings & Laboratories

Next we discussed our dream with Aaron Barron, a friend, also a critic and newspaper man. He saw the point—and the need for underwriters, since we ourselves did not have the money. He advised us to talk to the Charles S. Guggenheimers.

Soon, at a dinner at their home, I was sitting next to Mr. Guggenheimer. I told him of the success of Arnold's orchestral programs in Central Park, and in the light of this analogy, outlined our more far-reaching plan for the Stadium, including the fact that I had already gone so far as to get the option on it.

Mr. Guggenheimer's sister, Mrs. Philip Lewisohn, was the sister-in-law of Adolph Lewisohn. I told Mr. Guggenheimer it seemed logical now to enlist Adolph Lewisohn's help in extending the use of the Stadium beyond athletics into the realm of culture.

I shall never forget Mr. Guggenheimer's responsive verve. He said, "You must tell Minnie about this right away. She can get Adolph Lewisohn for you." Then turning to his wife he exclaimed: "Minnie, the Volpes have a wonderful idea. Listen to it!"

Mrs. Guggenheimer's reaction surpassed even that of her husband. She proved it immediately by arranging a dinner to bring us together with Mr. Lewisohn. I sat next to him. He was most charming—but absolutely out of tune with any suggestions about concerts. He kept changing the subject, and rather abruptly.

Mrs. Guggenheimer, keeping an ear to our conversation, would pointedly try to bring him back by saying: "Adolph, please listen to what Mrs. Volpe has to say. It is a wonderful idea, and I want you to hear it."

Then she would turn to me and say: "Go on, Mrs. Volpe, tell him what you have in mind."

But as soon as I said "concerts," his next sentence would be on something else. This lasted, almost like a game, right through the dessert and coffee, with the score all in Mr. Lewisohn's favor.

After dinner Mrs. Guggenheimer and I went up to her

room for a strategy conference. We were both discouraged. But she said comfortingly: "Don't give up; let's go down and try all over again!"

At last, late in the evening, I had a chance. I asked him if he would lend us his home for our first little meeting to discuss the concerts. He said he would have no objection to that. I told him that although I appreciated it, I would not accept his kindness unless he promised to be there himself. To get rid of me he said he would.

The very next morning I got his secretary to set a time when he would be free to attend.

Next, we invited Ossip Gabrilowitsch, whose name just then was especially prominent in New York musical news, to come to tell Mr. Lewisohn what Europe offered during the summer months, how each city had a "kursaal" for concerts, and of the festivals and so on. He was to provide Mr. Lewisohn with so vivid a picture it would be easy for him to project it to the Stadium. Others at that first meeting at the Lewisohn home, at 881 Fifth Avenue, were Dr. Storey, Louis Fehr, and Mr. and Mrs. Charles S. Guggenheimer.

Ossip Gabrilowitsch was always a good speaker, but on that occasion he outdid himself. In his gentle but eloquent voice, he spoke for half an hour. Breathing sincerity and conviction, he held his listeners with a persuasive magnetism I never saw him equal, except at the piano. The effectiveness of his presentation brought tears to my eyes. Twice I saw Arnold swallow a lump. Mrs. Guggenheimer was transported, and I could see she was anxious to get on with the job of clinching the objective. It looked so easy after Gabrilowitsch had done so well.

Then Mr. Lewisohn asked how much it would take to start. We replied: an underwriting of $10,000 for a tryout of two weeks.

After two hours of combing the details, Mr. Lewisohn announced he would give $500.

My ears were filled with a confused inner roaring—high-pitched and clangorous. Suddenly I realized the meeting was breaking up. Through the roaring I heard Mrs. Guggenheimer saying to me in a voice intended to be reassuring, not to worry, not to be disappointed, she "would handle Adolph for *that*."

Chapter XV

STADIUM CONCERTS—1918

IT WAS SHORTLY after the meeting at the Lewisohn home that Gabrilowitsch gave his series of concerts introducing him to American audiences as a symphony conductor.

Music lovers and socialites packed the performances, to hear him conduct or play as a soloist in concertos. He played as soloist the Mozart concerto in D minor, the Schumann concerto in A minor, and Franck's *Variations Symphoniques.* For each of these, he turned the baton over to Arnold. Although Arnold always conducted without score, I recall that on these occasions quite a point was made of his conducting accompaniments without one. The many conductors attending the performances hailed this as an unparalleled accomplishment of the concert stage.

But I also remember another matter of equal importance at the time. At the close of the first concert, Mr. Lewisohn came backstage to the artist's room to congratulate Gabrilowitsch, about whom he had now been informed. I had just said to myself: "He does learn these things so rapidly," when he took me aside and said: "I will raise my subscription to the Stadium Concerts to $1,000."

For five months Mrs. Guggenheimer and I worked. How we worked to raise the guarantees! It seemed that neither of us took time to put food into our mouths or to close our eyes. The concerts were incorporated. Arnold and I were included in the original corporation handling operations the first year.

We did not dream when we brought the idea to the Guggenheimers that we were making history in the advancement, appreciation, and growth of music in America. When we set to work there was no time for dreaming. So many things to do!

Arnold stepped briskly into preparation of programs. Mrs. Guggenheimer and I together called on everybody, it seemed. Otto Kahn was one of the men who suggested we enlist the interest of the younger men and women of taste and wealth. Mrs. Newbold Le Roy Edgar was the first woman we called on. She in turn interested Mrs. Charles Dana Gibson, and in turn Mrs. Gibson interested others. Suddenly everybody became interested and was ready to help. We soon had an admirable executive committee:

Mrs. Charles S. Guggenheimer, chairman; Mrs. Le Roy W. Baldwin, treasurer; and Mrs. Charles B. Alexander, Mrs. Newbold Le Roy Edgar, Mrs. Robert L. Gerry, Mrs. Charles Dana Gibson, Mrs. E. H. Harriman, Mrs. Thomas Hastings and Mrs. Charles H. Senff.

FIRST PROGRAM:

CITY COLLEGE STADIUM OPEN-AIR CONCERTS

Opening Night, Sunday Evening, June 23, 1918 at 8:30

STADIUM SYMPHONY ORCHESTRA

ARNOLD VOLPE, *Conductor*

METROPOLITAN OPERA HOUSE CHORUS

GIULIO SETTI, *Director;* ANNA FITZIU, *Soprano Soloist*

Program

PART I

MARCH—"Pomp and Circumstance" .... *Elgar*

SYMPHONY—"New World" *Dvorak*

PART II

OVERTURE—"William Tell" *Rossini*

ARIA—"Ritorna Vincitor" from "Aida" ...... *Verdi*

"Easter Song" from "Cavalleria Rusticana" *Mascagni*
Miss Anna Fitziu & Chorus

"AMERICAN REVEILLE"—
A Patriotic Fantasie *Arnold Volpe*
Anna Fitziu,
Orchestra & Chorus

PRELUDE .... *Orchestra*
(a) Tenting on the Old Camp Ground
(b) My Own United States
(c) Old Folks at Home
Anna Fitziu and Chorus

MARCH-SONG—"The American Reveille"
Orchestra and Chorus

ALLIED NATIONAL ANTHEMS:
England (The British Grenadiers)
Scotland (The Campbells Are Coming)
Ireland (St. Patrick's Day)
Wales (Men of Harlech)
Anzacs (Rule, Britannia)—Chorus
Italy (Marcia Reale)—Chorus
Belgium (La Brabanconne)
France (La Marseillaise)—Chorus

Star Spangled Banner—Chorus

IN CASE OF RAIN, PERFORMANCE WILL BE GIVEN IN THE GREAT HALL OF CITY COLLEGE, 139TH STREET AND CONVENT AVENUE

Soldiers and Sailors admitted Free

First concert, Lewisohn Stadium, June 23, 1918

ENGAGEMENT EXTRAORDINARY

Lexington Theatre

East 51st Street and Lexington Avenue

SUNDAY, AUGUST 21, 1921

8:15 o'Clock, P.M.

Gigantic Musica

Festival

Augmented Orchestra of 300 of New York's Selected

Largest Orchestra Ever Assembled in the History of

ARNOLD VOLPE, Conductor

Prices—25c, 50c, 75c

Under the Auspices

Musical Mutual

ENGAGEMENT EXTRAORDINARY

LEXINGTON THEA

East 51st Street and Lexington Avenue

Gigantic Musical F

Augmented Orchestra of 300 of New York's Selected Music

Largest Orchestra Ever Assembled in the History of Music

ARNOLD VOLPE, Conductor

ALBERTO BACHMAN, Concert Master

Program for Week Commencing Sunday, August 21, 1921

SUNDAY NIGHT

Wagner and Tschaikowsky

1—Meistersiger Vorspiel .... Wagner
2—Capriccio Italien .... Tschaikowsky
3—Prelude and Love Death Tristan .... Wagner
4—Overture 1812 .... Tschaikowsky
5—Prelude—"Lohengrin" .... Wagner
6—Third Movement from the Sixth Symphony .... Tschaikowsky
7—Overture—"Rienzi" .... Wagner
8—March Slave .... Tschaikowsky

MONDAY NIGHT

Italian Night in Memory of Enrico Caruso

Soloist—Emanuele Sarmiento, Italian Tenor

Il Miserere (In Memoriam)
1—Overture—"William Tell" .... Rossini
2—Fantasy—"La Boheme" .... Puccini
3—Aria.
4—Two Intermezzi from "The Jewels of the Madonna" .... Wolf-Ferrari
5—Fantasy—"Aida" .... Verdi
6—Dance of the Hours .... Punchielli
7—Fantasy—"Cavalleria Rusticana" .... Mascagni
8—Fantasy—"I Pagliacci" .... Leoncavallo

TUESDAY NIGHT

Russian Night

Soloist to be announced later

—Overture—"Romeo and Juliet"

WEDNESDAY

French Nig

Soloist—Madeleine MacG

1—Overture—"Phedre"
2—Suite—"Arlesienne"
3—Violin Solo—"Rondo Capric
4—Meditation
5—Rhapsody—"Espagna"
6—Suite—"Sylvia"
7—Soloist.
8—Fantasy—"Faust"
9—Suite—Scenes Neapolitains

THURSDAY NIG

Opera Night

Soloist to be announced

1—March—"Prophete"
2—Overture—"Mignon"
3—Fantasy—"Carmen"
4—Soloist.
5—Fantasy—"Cavalleria Rusticana"
6—March—"Tannhauser"
7—Fantasy—"Madame Butterfly"
8—Dance of the Hours
9—Aria.
10—Fantasy—"Aida"

FRIDAY NIGHT

Wagner Night

1—March—"Tannhauser"
2—Overture—"Rienzi"
3—Walters Prize Song from "Die M
4—Good Friday Spell
5—Siegfried's Rhine Journey
6—Prelude—"Lohengrin"
7—Prelude and Love Death from and Isolde"
8—Wotan's Farewell
9—Overture—"Tannhauser"

Gigantic Musical Festival given by augmented orchestra of 300 of New York's selected musicians under the direction of Arnold Volpe, 1921.

These were the names carried on the first program of the Stadium Concerts. For the record, it is noteworthy that Mr. Lewisohn's name did not appear. The Series was called the "City College Stadium Open-Air Concerts."

I will not attempt to portray all the action and work that went into the planning and production of that first program. A wonderful friend was Mrs. Julian Edwards, widow of the gifted composer. Through her efforts, her brother, Edward Siedle, of the Metropolitan Opera Company, became interested in the Stadium. He planned and built the platform for the orchestra at cost. Giulio Setti, director of the chorus of the Metropolitan, obtained the chorus for the lowest possible fee. For these three, special praise.

While all these and many other business and management essentials were going forward, Arnold had to figure out how in the world to put on seven performances with only two rehearsals. There was usually a soloist or two on every program, and many programs included presentations by the Metropolitan chorus. Only his thorough knowledge of every score enabled him to do it. Program planning in itself was a problem—in the absence of Wagner, Beethoven, Brahms, Bach or other Germans or Austrians.

Ninety soloists appeared in the first two summers. Anna Fitziu at the first concert sang a patriotic fantasie Arnold had arranged and entitled "American Reveille."

Special programs on the Fourth of July and other holidays brought some of the great stars to the Stadium to participate in the celebrations. There was the incomparable Schumann-Heink, grasping an American flag in her hand, singing our Anthem, with tears streaming down her cheeks, thinking, no doubt, of her own boys on the other side of the ocean. There were Ethel Barrymore, Margaret Matzenauer, and Rosa Ponselle who worked so enthusiastically with Arnold on special programs.

Operas were given in concert form under the choral conductor, Setti, with the entire Metropolitan Opera chorus. Saturday nights, with miscellaneous programs, were the most popular.

I have heard it thoughtlessly stated in recent times that none of the top ranking artists would appear at the Stadium in the first two years. I wish I could recall all ninety, but here is a partial list. When added to the names already mentioned, the list is, I am sure, large enough to reveal that the great of those times were included. Some of them were:

Florence Macbeth, Harold Bauer, Mana-Zucca, Alfred Megerlin, Edna Kellogg, Inez Barbour, Helen Stanley, John Powell, Marie Rappold, George Reimherr, Robert Maitland, Rudolph Reuter, Zana de Primo, Earl Tuckerman, Idelle Patterson, Olga Carrara, Mayo Wadler, Albert Janpolski, Forrest Lamont, Sascha Jacobsen, May Peterson, Lillian Eubank.

Percy Hemus, Samuel Gardner, Cecil Arden, Clarence Whitehill, Philip Gordon, Max Rosen, Victoria Boshka, Elias Breeskin, Nevada van der Veer, Reed Miller, Della Baker, Sada Cowen, Arthur Middleton, Adamo Didur, Ilja Schkolnik, Mary Jordan, Rafaelo Diaz, Giovanni Martino, Constance Balfour, Marie Tiffany, Marguerite Namara, Ernest Davis, Ernesto Berumen, Frank La Forge, Edna de Lima, Sue Harvard, Blanche da Costa, Alma Clayburgh, Donna Easley, and Blanche Arral.

They were times of high emotion, and among memories of nights especially intense arise tragi-comic pictures of huge, confused crowds fleeing in the rain. What scampering and sprinting when suddenly before the beginning of a program, the sky would darken and rain would begin to fall. All the equipment was rushed pell-mell to the Great Hall. Damp people, steamily smiling in good sportsmanship, would stand everywhere. In just a few minutes, with all the windows closed as the deluge dashed against the panes, how hot and sticky it got.

But mostly I remember the rise and sweep of the music through the open amphitheater, up to the acres of people, then on through the glow cast by the city, and higher ever higher, to the gently-shining stars pinned to the soft canopy of the summer night. In the Stadium, where all could come—all who hungered either for the balm or the inspiration of music—art transcended the worldliness of the city and transformed stones and humanity into something spiritual.

Art at the Stadium did many other things, too. Here was democracy, and confirmation of Arnold's belief that in the soul of all people lies a need for fine music—and a taste for it—far greater than any one in America had yet recognized. At least, no one else up to that time had bestirred himself to do as much about it.

Every musician who was in New York attended. Around the tables down front sat celebrities. Caruso was at the opening concert, and Frances Alda, and from another realm, Dr. and Mrs. Nicholas Murray Butler, and many others.

The audiences were huge, the ovations thunderous. The skeptics were indeed answered at the first season. A few contended stubbornly that the crowds were the result of "war fever" and that the patriotic aspects of the programs drew them. No one gave this fallacy any more thought than it deserved. It was clearly fine music—the masterpieces—the people came to hear.

When the season was over, we had some tangible results to show. There was no profit. No one had expected any. It had been undertaken by virtually all concerned as a deficit project. The disbursements were $41,247.27; the receipts were $31,959.26, making the deficit $9,288.01. The original guarantee of $10,000 we had asked for to carry the concerts for two weeks was more than enough to carry through for seven weeks.

We had squelched the pessimists on all important points. But before the finale of the season, we had achieved additional victories that, in all the ensuing years, have remained of importance. I quote from the New York *Herald*:

"In recognition of the work which Arnold Volpe and his orchestra are doing in the nightly concerts in the Stadium of the College of the City of New York, Adolph Lewisohn, who built the stadium and presented it to the college, gave a luncheon yesterday at Heather Dell Farm, his country home at Ardsley-on-Hudson, for Mr. Volpe. Others who have taken part in the concerts and several of the subscribers to them were at the luncheon.

"Among the guests were Mrs. Volpe, Mischa Elman, Miss Nina Elman, Miss Anna Fitziu, Mrs. Newbold Le Roy Edgar, Judge and Mrs. William H. Wadhams, Mr. and Mrs. Charles S. Guggenheimer, Mrs. Albert Sterner, Thomas Storey, Mr. and Mrs. Hans von Kaltenborn, Giulio Setti, Mr. and Mrs. Sigmund Spaeth, Mr. and Mrs. Louis Fehr, Mr. and Mrs. Fred C. Coppicus, Miss Emily Frances Bauer and Mr. and Mrs. Edward Siedle.

"Mr. Lewisohn made a brief speech, in which he said:

" 'We should crowd the Stadium each night to find in music surcease from toil of the day that is spent and inspiration for the days that are to come. Nor must we forget that we are providing inspiration and relaxation for the thousands of soldiers and seamen who are daily among us. We must let them know that at the Stadium they will find a welcome. They will go away more able to carry on the fight for liberty.

" 'If for no other reason, New York should see that these concerts are liberally supported. Today we honor Arnold Volpe and the committee of women who are making this work possible.' "

Others made many encouraging statements at the luncheon. The most interesting, to me, was Mr. Lewisohn's assertion that the concerts should be "liberally supported." It was advice he himself thereafter followed, through all the years.

His philanthropic interests extended into manifold fields—child welfare work, hospitals, et cetera. He was president of the Child Welfare League and the National Committee on

Prisons and Prison Labor. One of the concerts was held for the benefit of the latter and one for the eye clinic at Sing Sing. Arnold contributed his services, and Mr. Lewisohn was most appreciative.

Mr. Lewisohn gave several large dinner parties during the concert season at his Fifth Avenue home, notable for rich appointments, including the solid gold plates on which the dinners were served. In this residence he had a large gallery of paintings by old masters, as well as collections of modern French, English and American art, and many rare books.

He was 70 when the crowds at the Stadium opened his eyes to its use for aesthetic purposes, and suddenly this interest in music was expressed in a surprising personal activity. He took up singing lessons. He selected as his teacher Bertram Fox, a friend of ours he had met at a dinner party.

He already enjoyed dancing after dinner—at which he was good. Now, he added to his pleasure by giving a short recital, usually of the old German folk songs he loved. I remember the first in his repertoire was "Du, du liegst mir im Herzen."

During that first season so imbued with satisfaction at the immediate success of Arnold's music under the stars there were many dinners, luncheons, and teas honoring him. I remember especially a delightful tea given in their Brooklyn home by Mr. and Mrs. Hans Kaltenborn. The now eminent radio commentator was then connected with the *Brooklyn Eagle*. Even then, he always had a way of discerning significance in the earliest stages of a new movement.

"Meet me at the Stadium" became in one season an established New York slogan. When the concerts closed August 10, it was assumed by everyone that next summer they would again meet one another—and Arnold Volpe—there, probably at more and finer programs. He was known and beloved, now, by hundreds of thousands as a man with vision and a future.

Chapter XVI

STADIUM CONCERTS—1919

THE EFFECT of the Stadium Concerts' success upon some of the individuals concerned was unexpected. Instead of reducing our difficulties, the experience of the first summer multiplied them.

The new problems by no means were all artistic. Mrs. Charles S. Guggenheimer, chairman of the executive committee, left us. When first we saw "Minnie," as she came to be known, she was a quiet young woman and most attractive. One of her notable characteristics was shyness. The daughter of a substantial banker, with a cultured background, she had long been interested to some degree in music. At that time, she was one of Rubin Goldmark's pupils in composition. Otherwise, she had been absorbed in her home and her children and, naturally, was yet unknown to the public. I recall her attending one of our soirées, in December of 1917, in honor of the Flonzaley Quartet. She exhibited a notable reticence in meeting celebrities of the musical world.

Her interest in music was genuine. She was quick to realize the Stadium Concerts would give her opportunity to work for music and, as a public project, they would bring her into the civic limelight, a latent yearning until that time hidden by her shyness. She quickly threw off her demureness and proved her abilities in the succeeding years.

How she worked—and so ably—to help raise the guarantee to underwrite that initial success! As the two of us went from person to person that first year, we had virtually nothing tangible to describe. We had only Arnold's vision, beliefs and reputation to offer. It called for imagination and energy, and deservedly Mrs. Guggenheimer was made chairman of the executive committee.

In this position she was at once in the limelight. Before the season was half over, every musician had besieged her to help with whatever project lay close to his heart. A group of socially prominent women asked her to join them in starting a new orchestra for Edgar Varese. Dropping the Stadium Concerts at the end of the first year, she began to work instead for the National Symphony Orchestra of New York, which proved to be a short-lived venture and vanished as an entity at the end of a season.

Arnold and I, at least, had counted on her cooperation, not only to keep things together for the second season, but in the light of the demonstrated success of the initial venture, to help us expand.

When Mrs. Guggenheimer announced she was leaving the Stadium Concerts organization, she said to me:

"Don't worry, I won't take Adolph Lewisohn away from you."

And Mr. Lewisohn continued to work with us as shown in the letters below:

ADOLPH LEWISOHN & SONS
61 BROADWAY

New York, Feb. 15, 1919

Mrs. Arnold Volpe,
146 West 77th Street,
New York City.
Dear Mrs. Volpe:

When Dr. Storey comes to New York and will give matters attention, I think you and those who expect to work with you should have a meeting with him, at which I am also willing to be present, to see under what conditions the Stadium could be placed at the disposal of any undertaking which you expect to be able to carry out for next season. Of course the understanding will be that before final contract can be made financial guarantees will have to be added to same.

With kindest regards, I remain,
Your very truly,

Adolph Lewisohn

April 12, 1919

Mr. Alfred E. Seligsberg,
15 William Street,
New York City, N. Y.

My dear Mr. Seligsberg:

Mrs. Arnold Volpe advises me that the sum of Twenty-five Thousand Dollars ($25,000.) has been underwritten by Mr. Adolph Lewisohn, Mr. Sam Reckford, General Coleman Du Pont, Mr. A. D. Julliard, Mr. Edward F. Sanderson, Mr. Sam Lewisohn, and others for the purpose of guaranteeing a series of concerts which they hope to hold in the City College Stadium this coming summer.

Mrs. Volpe further advises me that you will act as attorney for these people and requests that I send you an outline of the agreement which the College will wish to execute with this Committee.

I am enclosing a rough copy of such an agreement. After you have indicated the proper designations with which we should fill out certain of the blank spaces in this agreement, the rough copy should be returned to me for submission to the Committee of the Board of Trustees which is in charge of the supervision of the Stadium and Field, under the chairmanship of Hon. H. J. Stroock. After receiving Mr. Stroock's approval of the agreement it will have to be written in permanent form and placed before the Corporation Counsel for approval as to form. In view of the fact that this form which I am sending you is practically the same as the form which we have been using for three or four summers, I assume that there will not be much difficulty or delay in securing the approval of the Trustees of the College of the City of New York, and the approval of the Corporation Counsel of the City of New York.

I expect to be out of the City until Saturday of this week. In case you desire information before Saturday, I can be reached care of the United States Interdepartmental Social Hygiene Board, Room 11, 1800 Virginia Avenue, N. W., Washington, D. C.,—or by telephone there—War Department, Branch 2883. During periods of my absence from the College, Assistant Professor Walter Williamson, the Acting Director of the College Stadium, may be of service to you.

Cordially yours,
Thomas A. Storey

When the time came to call on Mr. Lewisohn to tell him of the plans for a second season, for which a guarantee fund of

$25,000 was needed, I also had to give him the news that Mrs. Guggenheimer would not be with us. His answer was to tell me he would underwrite $12,500, or half the total amount, if I would raise the other half.

He said it with a cheerful twinkle in his eye. As I left, I pondered what that cheeriness meant. I finally decided it meant that he had enjoyed all the fruits of his connection with the Stadium Concerts—the dinners with musical celebrities and cultural leaders, the singing lessons, his after-dinner songs, and all. I decided, moreover, it meant he believed Arnold's demonstration of fine music for vast summer audiences was just the beginning and that he wanted to say so emphatically with a contribution of not less than fifty per cent of the backing.

There was still the problem of raising the other $12,500. This I did by going to Mrs. Helen Fountain and Samuel J. Reckford. The three of us enlisted the interest of the Music League of the People's Institute, which underwrote the remaining half. This carried with it the stipulation that the Stadium Concerts be given under auspices of the Institute.

Our first meeting under the new sponsorship took place in Mr. Lewisohn's downtown office. Arnold, Mr. Reckford and I stopped off on the way down for Alfred F. Seligsberg, attorney of the Metropolitan Opera House Company, whom Mr. Reckford had selected as attorney for the Stadium Concerts. As we started off in a taxi, I had a dreadful sense of foreboding. The first year, we had had such a simple little executive committee of women—such an unpretentious setup.

Now, there was a sizeable organization chart made up of little squares with connecting lines drawn to show how everything related, and the little squares were labeled "maintenance committee," "audition committee," "field committee," "finance committee," and "executive committee." Edward F. Sanderson's name, as Director of the People's Institute, was on the chart, and Sam A. Lewisohn, the son of Adolph Lewisohn, was in a little square of his own labeled "treasurer."

Prominently, up near the top, was the name of Adolph Lewisohn, I was glad to see, as honorary chairman. Alfred Seligsberg was chairman of the executive committee. At the top was Arnold Volpe, as conductor, indicating his responsibility.

But here we were, riding with an important attorney, not to a private home as we used to do for meetings the first year, but way downtown to a formal business office.

Perhaps, I thought as we rode along, I should not entertain fears about all this. The Stadium Concerts probably really had, in just one season, zoomed to the dimensions of big business and all its accoutrements. I remember turning to Mr. Seligsberg, however, and saying that now that we were working with the People's Institute and with such ramified committees, perhaps we ought to be equally businesslike and define and legally protect our rights as founders of the concerts.

I recall, too, how Mr. Reckford and Mr. Seligsberg laughed at me, and Mr. Seligsberg, in a pat-on-the-shoulder voice, said: "Why should you worry about anything; you have us and Mr. Lewisohn."

My fears vanished as we got down to work with final preparations. I was especially pleased by the dignity and clarity with which the forthcoming season was described in the pamphlet of announcement:

> SUMMER SYMPHONY CONCERTS FOR NEW YORK—New York is to have a summer season of the world's best orchestral and vocal music at the Stadium of the College of the City of New York. With the closing of the season proper our city has hitherto been deprived of its finest music at a time when music is particularly acceptable; that is, with the coming of the summer months. The season of eight weeks of concerts here outlined will thus provide an opportunity for many thousands of music lovers to spend their evenings in the open air, and to hear the works of the great masters under the moon and stars of the summer sky.
>
> The experiment with orchestral concerts in the open air made last summer in the Stadium proved most successful. It gained the warm appreciation of the public and the unanimous approval

of the press. The concerts were organized to place the best music within the reach of the general public during the summer months at the nominal admission of 25 and 50 cents. Over 100,000 people attended, the original season of two weeks was extended to seven weeks, and its closing was marked by an insistent demand for further concerts.

'The purpose of this movement,' as expressed by Andres de Segurola of the Metropolitan Opera Company, 'is to give adequate and dignified presentation of classic and modern music worthy of our great city, and to make this presentation independent and self-supporting. We believe that music will be one of the most important factors in social reconstruction following the war.'

Robert E. Ely, a director of the Civic Forum, adds: 'The plan for summer symphony concerts in New York is inspiring, and the Lewisohn Stadium is almost an ideal theatre for them. They will do much to relieve the torrid monotony of life that millions of people must lead in this city in July and August. They will express and strengthen the community spirit and they will bring spiritual refreshment to multitudes.'

An orchestra, composed of eighty musicians, under the direction of Arnold Volpe, has been chosen from the Metropolitan Opera House, the Philharmonic Society, and the New York Symphony orchestras. Arnold Volpe has been active in New York since 1902, as conductor of the Volpe Symphony Orchestra, the Young Men's Symphony Orchestra and the Municipal Orchestra.

The programmes will include symphonies and symphonic works by the great masters of all schools: Beethoven, Brahms, Schubert, Cesar Franck, Dvorak, Tschaikowsky, Rimsky-Korsakoff, Rachmaninoff, Borodin, Berlioz, Saint-Saens, Debussy, Dukas, Massenet, Liszt, Moussorgsky, Glazounoff, MacDowell, Hadley, Chadwick and others.

Vocal and instrumental soloists of prominence will assist on special nights, choral works will be given, and generally the arrangement of programmes will be as follows: Mondays and Thursdays—Symphony nights; Tuesdays and Fridays—Operatic nights; and Wednesdays, Saturdays and Sundays—Miscellaneous.

The founders of the Stadium Symphony Orchestra believe this movement to provide fine music for New York in the summer to have a distinct quality of civic value. They are of the opinion that it will make New York a pleasanter place in which to live and work, and they acknowledge their indebtedness to the authorities of New York City for concessions of lighting, licenses, permits and transportation facilities."

The 1919 season got off to a festive start. Rosa Ponselle was soloist. Mr. Lewisohn gave an opening address, and a new status for the "experiment" was revealed by the appearance on

STADIUM SYMPHONY ORCHESTRA
ARNOLD VOLPE, *Conductor*
Monday, June 30th, at 8:30 *p.m.,* 1919
SYMPHONY NIGHT
Soloist:
ROSA PONSELLE, *Soprano*
and Metropolitan Chorus

Program

PART I
Star-Spangled Banner
Opening Address by Mr. Adolph Lewisohn
SYMPHONY No. 5, C Minor.. *Beethoven*
Address by Hon. John F. Finley, *Commissioner of Education, State of New York.*
ARIA—"Pace, Pace, mio Dio," from "La Forza del Destino" *Verdi*
Rosa Ponselle

PART II
Capriccio Espagnol *Rimsky-Korsakov*
ARIA—"Suicidio," from Gioconda" *Ponchielli*
Rosa Ponselle
Marche Slave.. *Tschaikowsky*
Easter Prayer, from "Cavalleria Rusticana" ..*Mascagni*
Rosa Ponselle and Chorus

the program of Dr. John F. Finley, Commissioner of Education for the State of New York.

The series was scarcely under way when its increased degree of success was obvious. It was perfectly clear that the future of Arnold's pioneering venture was no longer problematical. Even the most reluctant skeptics could see that it was sound and good. There were some persons who began to view it as a "good thing," and by no means in an altruistic sense. Mr. Lewisohn was besieged by every friend, and every friend-of-a-friend, who knew a conductor, to give him a guest performance. Now that the act, so to speak, proved to be so good, everybody wanted to get into it.

Arnold, knowing by arduous experience the difficulties of giving seven performances with only the two rehearsals that the budget permitted, tried his best to explain it was impossible to do this with most guest conductors. In dealing with Mr. Lewisohn on this point, Arnold also fully realized the important considerations of public relations and diplomacy. The musicians of the orchestra, who after all were equally concerned with the quality of performances, were not so diplomatic. They called the guest conductors "pest conductors." And somehow in their loyalty to the high standards Arnold had set, they could not help but boil up from time to time, and unpleasant situations arose.

Another question came up. Now that the war was over, Arnold, wanting to return to purely aesthetic judgment of the symphonies to be played, included some of the compositions of German composers. He was opposed on every side within the Stadium Concerts organization. But when they were played, it was revealed that public tolerance in the realm of art was advanced far beyond what the pessimistic soothsayers had predicted.

The second season was especially notable, too, because Arnold made it another opportunity to perform a service for native music. He presented many works of American composers. This fine presentation of the compositions of Americans was appreciated, not only by the vast audiences, but by the composers. Many statements were made in person, thanking Arnold for the recognition and understanding interpretation, and he received numerous letters. I quote a typical one from A. Walter Kramer, written at Applejack Farm, Clapboard Ridge Road, Greenwich, Connecticut:

"I must write you a word of deep appreciation and thanks. Your interest in my *Symphonic Rhapsody* was very generous, and I cannot tell you how happy I was with the way you did it last evening.

"An old score—almost nine years old—one hasn't the same faith in as in a recent work. But I was delighted with the way it came out and glad that I could know that I did a score like that at nineteen and a half years of age.

"You have always been very kind to me in giving me a chance to be heard, and, as I told you last evening, I appreciate it all the more, because it is not usual in this world to get a chance from a conductor who knew one as a little boy playing viola in his orchestra on Sunday morning.

"Let me thank you again very heartily and sincerely for your kindness. With sincerest wishes to you and Mrs. Volpe, very cordially."

We had so many happy events of the summer to look back on. When Arnold's fiftieth birthday came on July 9, the orchestra surprised him completely backstage during the intermission by playing a fanfare to him and singing "Happy Birthday." Then the musicians presented him with a solid gold fountain pen and a large and beautifully ornate wreath. As a finale to the celebration, a glorious evening followed in our home at a supper to which I had invited many distinguished guests and the entire personnel of the orchestra.

When the season was over and all the results were summarized, every major phase added up to a complete success: audiences had been enthusiastic, critics were laudatory, and the conclusive arithmetic at the box office showed attendance and income had doubled. Arnold and I were, of course, gratified. The season had been a week longer than the year before, and the programs more difficult. But the people had been more appreciative, and there had been more of them listening.

The success of the season was delightfully reviewed by the speakers at a testimonial dinner given in Arnold's honor at the Hotel Astor, October 6, 1919. With dignified simplicity the souvenir menu said: "In appreciation of his work at the Lewisohn Stadium during the summer of 1919."

The Committee was:

Adolph Lewisohn, *Honorary Chairman*
Andres de Segurola, *Toastmaster*
Henry De Forest Baldwin
Harold Bauer
Sada Cowen
Mrs. L. R. De Cravioto
Mrs. Julian Edwards
Mrs. Helen Fountain
Anna Fitziu
Ossip Gabrilowitsch
Margaret Matzenauer
Rosa Ponselle
Mrs. Arthur M. Reis
Samuel J. Reckford
Marie Rappold
Edward F. Sanderson
Alfred F. Seligsberg
Helen Stanley
Dr. Thomas A. Storey

SPEAKERS

Mr. Rubin Goldmark
Mrs. Julian Edwards
Mr. Adolph Lewisohn

ARTISTS

Mme. Marie Rappold
Mr. Samuel Gardner

Arnold gave it an additional significance by insisting that Professor Auer share the honor with him. What an impressive experience it was to have his old teacher beside him, as high thanks were expressed for the advancement made in American musical life. The speeches were hearty, and in praising every aspect, most thorough.

Andres de Segurola of the Metropolitan Opera House was toastmaster, and Rubin Goldmark made an excellent speech.

Arnold paid deep tribute to Professor Auer, who in turn spoke delightfully of his pupil.

During his speech Arnold said something which pleased me very much: "My deepest thanks on this occasion to one who to me is friend, comrade, guide, counsellor, inspirer, conductor, in whose domestic orchestra I am always proud to play second fiddle, my wife, Marie Volpe."

Sometimes, after a season is over, after the last note has been played and goodbyes have been said, and the seats are empty and the charwomen come in, a formal dinner at a later date comes as an anticlimax. But not so with this one.

We were of course sorry that Mr. Lewisohn had to send a telegram of regret, but we were pleased by his statements of good wishes.

The evening built to a fine climax, and Arnold and I were exceedingly happy as we rode home afterward. Everyone had been so kind. And we had been so gullible.

Chapter XVII

STADIUM CONCERTS—1919-1920

EARLY ON THE MORNING after the testimonial dinner, I received a telephone call from our kind friend and constant well-wisher, Mrs. Philip Lewisohn.

She told me the newspapers the next day would carry an announcement for which Arnold and I should be prepared. She could not bear to have us get the first news from the papers, she said. It would be a shock. The papers would announce that the following summer Walter Henry Rothwell would conduct the Stadium Concerts.

It was there, the next day; that is, that much of the story—that Mr. Rothwell, not Arnold, would conduct. When would the *rest* of the story come out? What *was* the rest? We did not know. Who *did* know?

That was how Arnold found out that he had been robbed of his greatest life-work. He was a broken-hearted man. He kept asking why—how—it could have happened. He reviewed every action, every detail of the season—every action, every detail of the season before. He could find no clue. He kept going over it all: the attendance and the receipts had doubled; the entire press and the public were behind him. Over and over and over he sifted his memory, examining everything everyone had said or done at any time. He could find not one shred of evidence—nothing that betrayed the cause.

Again and again the recollection of the applauding audiences rang in our ears—and those speeches "in appreciation of his work" at the dinner.

There must have been many persons at that dinner who knew what the papers were going to say in less than 48 hours. Arnold was beginning to question his sanity. This couldn't have happened! The dinner couldn't have happened! This

Flonzaley Quartet, 1917

Farewell dinner honoring Mme. Sembrich, Feb. 7, 1909, among those pictured are Mme. Sembrich and her husband, Professor Stengel, Mr. and Mrs. Gustav Mahler, Mr. and Mrs. Henry Krehbiel, Mr. and Mrs. W. J. Henderson, Mr. and Mrs. Walter Damrosch, Mr. and Mrs. Ignace Paderewski, Enrico Caruso and Daniel Frohman.

Dinner honoring Arnold Volpe after the second season of the Stadium Concerts, October 6, 1919. Andres De Segurola was toastmaster and the speakers included Rubin Goldmark, Mrs. Julian Edwards and Adolph Lewisohn. Artists on the program were Mme. Marie Rappold and Samuel Gardner. On the dinner committee were Henry De Forest Baldwin, Harold Bauer, Sada Cowen, Mrs. L. R. De Cravioto, Mrs. Julian Edwards, Mrs. Helen Fountain, Anna Fitziu, Ossip Gabrilowitsch, Maragaret Matzenauer, Rosa Ponselle, Mrs. Arthur M. Reis, Samuel J. Reckford, Marie Rappold, Edward F. Sanderson, Alfred F. Seligsberg, Helen Stanley, Dr. Thomas A. Storey.

The Evening Post.
New York, Monday, March 20, 1911.

The New York Press
DAILY EDITION
New York, Monday, March 20, 1911.

The World

Volpe Symphony Season Ends With a Demonstration

Mr. Volpe Saluted and Presented With a Wreath
Mr. Morrison Reports That There Is No Deficit and That Prospects ... Next Year

THE EVENING MAIL

LAST CONCERT OF VOLPE SYMPHONY ORCHESTRA

Two Movements of a Foote Suite and the Fifth Beethoven Symphony Performed—New York Symphony Concert at the New Theatre.

Heinemann at Volpe Symphony Society's Concert

The World.

Volpe Symphony Orchestra Heard in Fine First Concert

Leader Directs His Young Men Through Long Programme Without a Score, to His Own, His ...

VOLPE ORCHESTRA OPENS FOURTH CONCERT SEASON

SYMPHONY ORGANIZATION IS HEARD IN "DAS HEXENLIED"

NEW FARWELL WORK PLAYED BY VOLPE

Unanimous Verdict of the New York Critics on the Success of the VOLPE SYMPHONY ORCHESTRA Concert, January 9th, 1910

NEW YORK SUN.

NEW YORK EVENING MAIL.

MONDAY, JANUARY

The World

THE VOLPE ORCHESTRA PLAYS CESAR FRANCK

French Master's Little Known Symphony Is Feature of an Attractive Concert.

By Reginald de Koven.

VOLPE ORCHESTRA AT CARNEGIE HALL

THIS ORGANIZATION OF YOUNG PLAYERS GIVES A MOST CREDITABLE PERFORMANCE.

AMERICAN MUSIC AT THE VOLPE CONCERT

Volpe Symphony Orchestra

The Sun.
WEDNESDAY, NOVEMBER 29, 1911.

VOLPE ORCHESTRA CONCERT

NOT MUCH CHANCE FOR PURE AMERICAN MUSIC

Edgar Stillman Kelley Says That This Country Has Little to Offer in the Way of Folklore or Folksong Upon Which to Build ... Overture to Be Played by the Volpe

From New York papers, 1911

Various New York Programs

story in the papers couldn't be true!

Suddenly, I realized that at the October 6th dinner there were indeed some who, for quite a while, had known this blow would fall. I recalled a letter from Dr. Storey that I had received in the middle of September, saying that he had "been asked very recently" if the college had given me an option on the Stadium for the next summer. As a normal business courtesy he had agreed to inform me.

If there had been dissatisfaction with Arnold on the part of any or all of those committees, why hadn't they invited Arnold to a hearing? No, it couldn't be that. It couldn't be dissatisfaction. Around and around our wondering, guessing, speculating minds raced in baffled striving to find the cause, until our weary brains staggered.

No one who knew would talk. Soon, Mrs. Guggenheimer telephoned, not to talk about *why* this had happened, as I understood it, but to suggest getting together to discuss as an aftermath what could be done for Arnold.

In my benumbed state, I could see no purpose, unless it could be revealed what had been behind the action. I said: "What's done is done! But remember, every stone in that Stadium will cry out for what has been done to the Volpes."

I can scarcely describe Arnold's agonies. We reviewed the whole situation and summed it up: there was that closing night at the concerts, with Arnold on the podium, the hero of music-loving New York. Next, the night of the testimonial dinner—praised and honored. Then, that incredible morning on which he was left, except for Mrs. Philip Lewisohn's thoughtful warning, to read in the papers that he had been replaced.

Intellectually, as a scholarly musician and perfectionist who was his own sternest taskmaster, he knew that the concerts had been good. On this point his morale had been untouched.

In all his career, there had been so much giving of himself for musical ideals. With the ideal of orchestral training for youth, when none was available in America, he had founded the Young Men's Symphony Orchestra; with the ideal of providing symphonic opportunity for young professionals, he had founded the Volpe Symphony Orchestra. He had fostered the compositions of American composers, and incited an interest in American works, giving them emphasis in his programs, when virtually all others ignored them.

He had long discerned the unnourished hunger of the public for fine music, irrespective of economic class, and yearned for the chance to feed it generously. Arnold's alert idealistic eyes, and none other's, had first seen those acres of empty seats in Mr. Lewisohn's stadium as a setting for symphonies, and we had first gathered the key people for an organization and shown them how to fill those seats with lovers of music.

Of course, it could be said that as a career musician he had been paid $28.57 to conduct each concert. But even behind the barricade of secrecy with which the concert committee had guarded itself, we were sure his salary had not been the issue.

No, we decided, there was something more significant than that. Certainly, nevertheless, it had been behind our backs that Arnold's idealism had been stabbed. I have never seen a man so crushed, so disillusioned. It was not only his love of striving for the cause of music that had been cut down, but now he held grave doubts as to the integrity of those who, as respected co-workers, but a few days before, seemingly, had been sharing his altruism.

The condition of his thoughts turned so morbid that I watched him constantly for fear of suicide. But to mend his damaged faith in humanity, he turned to faith in God. Arnold, who had never until then been deeply interested in religion, turned to prayer, and it restored his courage. During all this time, neither of us had said anything publicly about what had happened. The newspapers merely carried the fiction "Arnold Volpe has withdrawn from the Stadium Concerts."

In the spring, when the plans for 1920 had been announced, I could not help writing Mr. Lewisohn a letter in which I breathed fire and let off steam—to an extent I would never allow myself again. It was a letter filled with bitterness, measure for measure for our aching hurt. It showered brimstone on the committee and Mrs. Guggenheimer and Mr. Lewisohn in particular—which also I would not do again.

The tone of my unhappy letter was accusatory; its chief purpose was to try to learn, at last, why Arnold had been robbed of the legitimate fruits of his labor, why he had been treacherously stabbed in the dark. It was filled with Why! Why! Why!

Mr. Lewisohn's reply contained some interesting statements, but none that answered our "Why!"

He said he regretted the tone of my letter—which was natural. He went on to say: "While it is true that you suggested the Stadium for summer concerts two years ago, my ambition for years has been to give the people of New York music at popular prices."

The first part of the sentence contained no news. But the latter part was startling, and again my head was filled with clamor and roaring, a feeling I remembered first at the meeting in his house, when at the conclusion of Gabrilowitsch's talk and the long explanation, Mr. Lewisohn had proffered $500.

I searched the letter for any inkling of what lay behind the committee's action toward Arnold. Mr. Lewisohn wrote:

"I suggested that Mr. Volpe be engaged to conduct at least part of the concerts for the coming season as I desired to give him every consideration and I know Mrs. Guggenheimer also wished to bring about the same results, but it was finally decided by a majority in interest to engage Mr. Rothwell for this season."

I scanned the letter again and again, especially the phrase "decided by a majority in interest." Officially, this would be the executive committee. I was a member of the executive committee and had received no notice of any meeting to discuss the engagement of Mr. Rothwell for the following season.

Mrs. Guggenheimer was not a member of the executive committee, nor, indeed, of any part of the Stadium Concerts organization. Officially, that year, she was busy with matters of the National Symphony Orchestra of New York.

As to my use of the word treachery, Mr. Lewisohn wrote: "I am sure that on reflection you will realize your first impression has been mistaken." His letter was dated March 16, 1920.

As Mr. Lewisohn suggested, we tried to reflect, but there was nothing new offered for reflection, and our stunned and baffled minds, even six months after the shock, were still not sufficiently recovered for any process so orderly.

We perused Mr. Lewisohn's phrase: "I desired to give him every consideration." He had written this letter only about two years after Gabrilowitsch, Mrs. Guggenheimer and I had urged him into cooperation in effecting Arnold's idea. Now, somehow, step by step, he was in a position to give the artist-creator "every consideration."

As I have said, Arnold and I did not discuss the situation publicly. But within the profession—among conductors and other artists whose careers depended on dealing with organizations and committees and individuals of power—many questions were asked. They came to us with questions. We could tell them privately what had happened, but we could not tell them why, for still we didn't know. Nor could they tell us.

But if you had been at gatherings of artists in those days, you would have heard much discussion. There was a general scrambling of artists to attorneys, a sudden interest in contract law, in ways and means to see it didn't happen to them. One conductor, calling on Arnold to sympathize, stated: "Volpe, this will never happen to me." He had just changed the name of his band to include his own name, a protective device that has since been effectively used by many other artists.

The concerts for the summer of 1920 began auspiciously with Mrs. Guggenheimer again in the harness, and Mr. Rothwell on the podium.

In a few weeks we received a call from Mr. Seligsberg. Things were not going satisfactorily. Yes, the committee had worked hard, and the organization was fine. But the public was not interested. Would Arnold come back for a week—at $1,000? That was five times his weekly salary of the year before.

It was a painful question. It was like a cautery in an unhealed wound. Yet, if the Stadium Concerts were in trouble—if the audiences wanted his music—

"What would you do, Mr. Seligsberg?"

"I would certainly not accept," Mr. Seligsberg said.

That was that. We took his advice.

"By the way, Mr. Seligsberg," I asked, "do you recall a conversation we had last year in the taxi going down to Mr. Lewisohn's office for the first meeting of the Stadium Concerts committee? Do you remember my asking whether a legal understanding about our rights as originators and conductor was not advisable? Do you recall your answer? Your laugh?"

How I wished I had insisted on legal protection. How differently things might have worked out had I followed my premonition. In the interval of his silence I almost asked if he had received any reports that the stones of those vacant seats in the Stadium cried out.

At the end of the pause, Mr. Seligsberg said: "You can't fight millions."

With that enigmatical reply, we were still no closer to an answer to "Why was this done to us?"

Mr. Rothwell's contract was not renewed for the next season.

It was four years before we had our explanation of the committee's action aginst us. Meanwhile, Arnold's work had taken us to Kansas City. We came back to New York for a summer visit. We were staying with friends on the New Jersey coast. A telephone call came from Berthold Neuer, President of the Knabe Piano Company and an old friend. It was like a thunderbolt.

"Marie," he asked, "will you and Arnold join me at the opening of the Stadium Concerts tonight?"

Never was an invitation to "Meet me at the Stadium" received with such astonishment. Cautiously, I approached my husband. We swallowed hard, shed some tears. Arnold said: "If you can go, then I can go, too."

We went. The first to greet us was "Minnie." In her well-carrying voice, she told everybody: "Here are the people responsible for these concerts."

Hearing that we were spending the week-end on the Jersey Coast near her home, she invited us to dinner. After much hesitation and discussion with Arnold, we accepted. At the dinner, besides Mr. and Mrs. Guggenheimer, were also Mr. Guggenheimer's fine mother, Mrs. Randolph Guggenheimer, and Mrs. Philip Lewisohn. We had a round of recollections of the old days. However, it was not an easy experience.

Adolph Lewisohn was not there. He was waiting to see us, Mrs. Guggenheimer told us, at his own place nearby. After dinner, Mrs. Guggenheimer and Arnold and I went over. We found him standing on the lawn. He seemed pleased to see us.

He told us that William Andrew Clarke, Jr., of Los Angeles, had sent $10,000 to the committee so that Mr. Rothwell could be the conductor of the Stadium Concerts. We understood the reasoning behind Mr. Clarke's offer. A summer at the Stadium, in the wake of Arnold Volpe, would enhance Mr. Rothwell's reputation as conductor of the Los Angeles Philharmonic Orchestra.

That, then, was what "those in interest" had done.

I said to Mr. Lewisohn: "And so you sold Arnold Volpe's birthright for $10,000."

Mr. Lewisohn did not reply.

When Mr. Lewisohn divulged the deal, Mr. Rothwell no longer had need of its benefits, and our regard for those responsible for this great injustice to us had long been dead.

The Stadium Concerts went on; the pioneering had been virile.

Mrs. Guggenheimer went on; she never unbuckled herself again from the harness she wears with such distinction.

Mr. Lewisohn is dead.

Arnold Volpe, too, is dead, and I have gone on alone to put these facts on record in justice to Arnold's memory as a creator and an artist of integrity.

Chapter XVIII

REMINISCENCE

OUR LIFE IN NEW YORK—from our wedding day, in April, 1902, was filled with delightful friendships and colorful associations.

For twenty years, except for the brief trips to Europe, and journeys to Washington and Philadelphia in connection with Arnold's work, we scarcely left the city. Connections with so many prominent musicians and patrons of music of those days filled those two decades with events that are pleasant to look back upon.

The farewell dinner for Mme. Sembrich in February, 1909, brought together an outstanding assemblage of musical artists. At the guests' table with Mme. Sembrich and her husband Professor Stengel, sat Mr. and Mrs. Gustav Mahler, Mr. and Mrs. Henry Krehbiel, Mr. and Mrs. W. J. Henderson, Mr. and Mrs. Walter Damrosch and Mr. and Mrs. Ignace Paderewski.

At each table sat a music critic or other prominent newspaper man. During the dinner, artists at the various tables arose and sang passages from Mme. Sembrich's repertoire. After dinner, there was a reception and dancing. Paderewski played a waltz, as Mme. Sembrich and Caruso danced. It was an unforgettable occasion in homage to a superb career.

When Caruso and Arnold were introduced, Caruso, upon hearing the name Volpe, automatically addressed Arnold in Italian, telling him how proud he was that a fellow countryman had achieved such a successful career. Arnold replied in Italian, but had to explain that although his name was Italian, he was Russian. Caruso seemed a bit disappointed, but later in the evening selected Arnold as the subject of one of his famous caricatures—a splendid one.

The early meetings of the Bohemians, of which Arnold was a member, were impressively informal occasions at Luchow's restaurant, on Fourteenth Street. The music was never a concert, but usually unprepared. Everyone sat around eating sandwiches and drinking beer. The great Joseffy, founder; Rubin Goldmark, the first president; Franz Kneisel, who became the second president, and other oldtimers, who loved to make music for the sake of music, gave many unusual programs.

I remember the last two ladies' nights especially. Alma Gluck Zimbalist looked particularly beautiful in a black velvet dress at one of them. At the last one Arnold and I attended, about 400 were awaiting the belated arrival of Caruso, the guest of honor, when, instead, came the announcement of his serious illness.

Many members of the Bohemians became members of the later Beethoven Association, although their activities were quite different.

The Beethoven Association originated from meetings of a number of prominent artists, all old friends, who were brought together during the summers of 1916 and 1917, because of World War I conditions. They were of many different nationalities, and it was their hope that a series of concerts given in the spirit of artistic fraternity might effectively help restore good international relations. Harold Bauer prepared a proposal of this nature, and Arnold was one of those invited to join. Soon after, he became a director in the Association.

The spirit of the Association was expressed in the concerts, for which the members rehearsed and played solely for their pleasure and the further objective of turning over the receipts to projects of general musical interest.

Many of our friendships grew out of the activities of the Volpe Symphony Orchestra. One to which I want particularly to pay tribute was the House of Steinway—Fred Steinway, Theodore Steinway, Mr. Reidemeister and Mr. Urchs—in fact everybody, including the doorman, was our friend.

They never said no; they not only supplied us with pianos, but contributed generously to the orchestra. When we opened our school, the Volpe Institute, Mr. Reidemeister asked how many pianos we needed. I told him five. They were there the next day, without even cartage charges.

Among our most loyal patrons were Dr. and Mrs. Henry Clarke Coe. Dr. Coe was one of the leading physicians of New York, and they enjoyed entertaining lavishly for musicians. At one of their soirées for Eugene Ysaye, in 1913, the guests came in costumes of the Eighteenth Century. It was a memorable sight, when around tables decorated in that period, the guests assembled in beautiful costumes and white wigs. Ysaye, who added to the evening by playing, evoked one of the warmest tones ever produced from a violin.

Another patroness who often entertained after the concerts of the Volpe Symphony Orchestra, in her large home on West 75th Street, was Mrs. H. H. Hendricks. Also the George Bernards who proved their friendship to us innumerable times.

With an idea of my own, I once involved myself in an exciting experience, unknown to Arnold. I had conceived the idea of interesting the Progressive Party in sponsoring orchestral concerts in New York. It was after Theodore Roosevelt's presidency, and he was then connected with *The Outlook* magazine.

Mrs. Frederick Nathan, President of the Consumers League of Women, who was responsible for many improvements in conditions for working girls in retail stores, was a continuous supporter of the Volpe Symphony Orchestra, and I knew she was well acquainted with Mr. Roosevelt.

She arranged an appointment. It was the only time I recall being nervous in meeting a prominent personality. Mr. Roosevelt was "Deelighted" when we met. He looked deep into my eyes, changed glasses twice, and seemed to be trying to read my soul. At last, when he seemed to be satisfied I was all right, we both relaxed and talked for a quarter of an hour or more.

He was well acquainted with Arnold's work and liked the idea of the concerts. The following day, Mrs. Nathan received a letter from him saying he would gladly endorse such a movement for the Progressive Party, adding: "There is no man better fitted in New York to conduct such programs than Arnold Volpe."

When I came home with the news, terribly excited, Arnold threw up his hands and said: "What will you do next?"

I had already begun to form committees, when I spoke to John C. Freund and others well known in the musical world. They all discouraged me, in effect advising me: "Why drag Arnold Volpe, a fine musician, into politics, something he could never cope with!" I could see their reasoning and gave up the idea.

One evening, a very tall, quiet-voiced man came to our home to confer with Arnold. So very tall, he seemed the original reason for the word towering, and he was most impressive of manner. Count Tolstoi he was, a son of Count Leo Tolstoi, author of *Anna Karenina,* and far into the night he and Arnold discussed what music might be written for a dramatization of his father's immortal novel. The details I never learned, for all of the conversation was in Russian. Arnold gave it serious consideration. But finally he decided he could not undertake it, for it was at a time when he was pressed urgently by other demands.

A gourmet memory is the spaghetti dinner with the Alessandro Boncis, before his appearance with the Volpe Symphony Orchestra in January, 1911. The meal was prepared and served by their famous Italian chef in their spacious apartment in the Ansonia Hotel. The main dish, of course, was spaghetti, and it was served on one of the largest platters ever seen, topped with a ravishing sauce and more chicken livers than I ever believed to exist in the world. Arnold and I tried to twist the spaghetti around the fork with the aid of a spoon.

But we laughingly admitted a great deal more practice was needed for us than even that immense quantity of spaghetti provided.

We first met Mary Garden as a result of a benefit concert given by the Volpe Symphony Orchestra, with Johanna Gadski as soloist, for the German Sailors Home, in March, 1912. It was the first time Mary Garden had heard Arnold conduct, and after the concert she expressed her enthusiasm through Berthold Neuer with an invitation to tea.

Although I contended that Mary Garden was not interested in the conductor's wife, Arnold insisted I go with him. She was most gracious and very beautiful with that lovely reddish-auburn hair. When we met fifteen years later, in Miami, she was still most attractive, and remembered and listed every number Arnold played at the Gadski concert.

In 1916, when "Roxy" Rothafel was first planning a motion picture theater, the Strand, with a large symphony orchestra, he negotiated with Arnold for about three months. Together they spent many evenings dreaming and planning to bring the best symphonic music to the masses at the price of a movie. It all seemed to be going along smoothly until the time came to work out the specific contract with Arnold and actually plan the programs. One night we stayed at "Roxy's" house until nearly 2 o'clock in the morning.

As we left, I noticed Arnold seemed to be much disturbed. He could never hide his emotions from me. The next morning we talked it all over, and he finally turned to me with tears in his eyes.

"Marie," he said, "do you want me to sell my soul? I know this means a great deal of money, more comfort for you and the children, but is *this* what I have been working for all my life? I can't do this."

I went quietly to the telephone and called "Roxy," telling him Arnold regretted he could not accept the position. In the following years, I often wondered whether that decision was wise. Before long some of our best musicians were connected with movie houses, bringing good music to the masses.

At the time of my husband's death, I could not help recalling these episodes. It might have made our life a bit easier—during Arnold's lifetime—and afterward. But I am grateful that I never influenced him to sacrifice his high standards of music or ideals for the sake of the almighty dollar.

In the summer of 1916, we took a cottage at Far Rockaway, Long Island. After we moved in, we found that Anna Fitziu had a large house right across the way. Such fun it was all summer, when the Vernon Stiles, de Segurola, the Leon Rothiers and so many others visited either across the street or with us. I don't think there ever was another artist who could sing *The Two Grenadiers* in French as Rothier did—and still does. I had the rare privilege of studying under him for six months, when I expected to make singing a career.

Another rendezvous for artists we enjoyed was Eugene Bernstein's house on West 70th Street. Many, like Chaliapin, Didur, and a long list of others, met there.

At Mark Fanaroff's home there were informal Sunday chamber music evenings, where one often met members of the Kneisel Quartet and others solely interested in chamber music. Mr. Fanaroff was a splendid violinist, and Vera, his wife, had been one of his pupils. Later, they both taught at the Institute of Musical Art, later joined to the Juilliard School of Music.

It was there we heard a nephew of Mrs. Fanaroff, the boy prodigy, Abram Chasins. Arnold predicted the fine future he certainly fulfilled, and Abram in later years played several times with Arnold and the University of Miami Symphony Orchestra. He was the first one to start a fund for the orchestra.

Another young pianist we admired was Leo Ornstein, one of the prides of Mrs. Thomas Tapper, wife of the educator and lecturer. She was a splendid piano pedagogue and a dear friend. Ornstein made his debut with the Volpe Symphony Orchestra at the New Amsterdam Theater, in 1911. Mrs. Tapper, his teacher, considered him one of the greatest talents of the period.

It was at the home of her genial teacher, William Thorner, that we met Rosa Ponselle, a year before her debut at the Metropolitan Opera. What fun we had celebrating a jolly New Year's Eve together, with Rosa at the piano, and she and her sister, Carmella, singing duets from their vaudeville repertoire.

Another good friend was Julia Culp; and, until he left to head the San Francisco Symphony Orchestra, Alfred Hertz also was a frequent visitor with us.

Among singers, there were so many good friends. David Bispham introduced my sister, Henriette, at her first public appearance when she was but sixteen. It was a large charity affair. Mr. Bispham, with his renowned diction and glorious voice, recited *The Raven* with piano accompaniment, then led Henriette to the platform, introducing her as "a very gifted and promising young pianist."

Margaret Matzenauer was one of the greatest artists at the Metropolitan Opera. How I used to enjoy the *kaffee klatches* at her parents' home on Central Park West! Others we so much enjoyed were Albert Reiss, Otto Goeritz and Marie Mattfeld.

The beautiful Martha Atwood, another fine Metropolitan Opera artist, introduced Arnold's song, *Ici Bas,* and sang it on many programs—and later on the radio.

Ballet—especially the Russian ballet—had intrigued Arnold ever since his student days in St. Petersburg. His interest brought about a fascinating friendship with Michel Fokine and his beautiful wife, Vera Fokina, with whom Arnold was associated in a number of performances at the Stadium, in 1927.

Fokine was a most interesting man, deeply engrossed in his work, and not easily satisfied. There was perfect understanding between him and Arnold, however, and the performances, therefore, were splendid. Arnold would attend many rehearsals in the Fokine studio with only piano accompaniment, studying the dances in order to become thoroughly familiar with every step before conducting the orchestral rehearsals.

After one of these private rehearsals, we were invited to remain for a Russian dinner. The Fokines' servants formerly were officers of the Russian army, who had escaped from Bolshevism with nothing but their lives and the clothes on their backs. For the time being, they accepted any kind of work others could give them in order to eat.

The dinner was amazing, not only because of these towering servants. There must have been twenty courses. I had not known there were that many different Russian dishes. Arnold had a wonderful nostalgic time talking Russian and enjoying all these recipes of his native land.

After dinner we went upstairs to the Fokines' studio, where Arnold, to a waltz he had composed and dedicated to Mme. Fokina, danced with her. I shall never forget how I tried to get up enough courage to dance with the great Fokine. But I never did.

Nor shall I ever forget another incident of quite another sort with the Fokines. It was at their performance in the Metropolitan Opera House, Philadelphia. Arnold had gone down from New York early in the day to conduct the final rehearsal in the afternoon. I went down that evening just a little before curtain time. When I went backstage to see Arnold, he was in the midst of an excited discussion with Fokine. I sensed there was something wrong, but had no idea what it was, for the torrent of exclamations was all in Russian.

I asked what the trouble was. They were reluctant to tell me. I insisted on knowing. Finally, after conferring on the wisdom of telling me, Arnold said: "Marie, Mme. Fokina's maid is about to give birth to a child. Can you help? She is in Mme. Fokina's dressing room."

This dressing room was also widely known in Philadelphia as Caruso's dressing room. I rushed in. Mme. Fokina stood ready to go on, costumed in all the flimsy tulle for the Swan number. I almost had to push her out—just in the nick of time

—as the baby was about to be born. I had been called upon to do almost everything under the sun, it seemed, but this was to be an entirely new experience for me. I called an ambulance and did what I could. When the doctor arrived, mother and baby were doing very nicely.

The word immediately spread through the entire opera house—somewhat confusedly: "Baby born in Caruso's dressing room!"

As we returned to New York together—Sol Hurok, the impresario, the Fokines, Arnold and I—what fun they had with me! Every time I looked up, they were ready with more witty teasing over my role as emergency midwife, which I had played in an evening gown. Even as recently as two years ago, when I was on a visit to New York, Mr. Hurok was recalling the old days with the Fokines and, of course, the episode of the backstage childbirth.

How often, all the old memories are relived—the great and the small ones, the impressive moments and those merely amusing—for down through the years the good friends have remained to remind me of all those treasured days.

What good fortune it was to have shared with Arnold such a wealth of associations and friendships in the world of great artists, who through their art, and as much through their brilliant personalities, have given so much to life that is pleasant and good to remember.

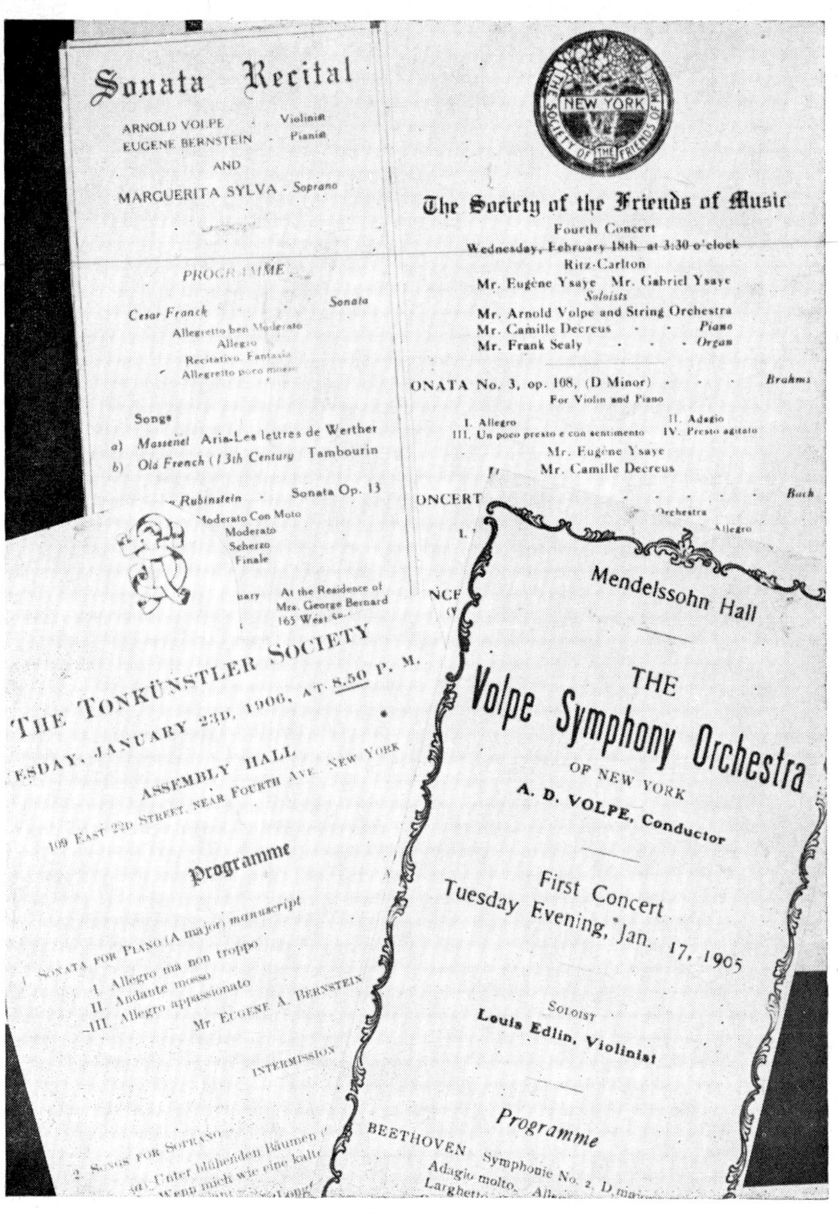

Sonata Recital
ARNOLD VOLPE - Violinist
EUGENE BERNSTEIN - Pianist
AND
MARGUERITA SYLVA - Soprano
Cesar Franck Sonata
Allegretto ben Moderato
Allegro
Recitativo. Fantasia
Allegretto poco mosso
Songs
a) Massenet Aria-Les lettres de Werther
b) Old French (13th Century Tambourin
Rubinstein Sonata Op. 13
Moderato Con Moto
Moderato
Scherzo
Finale
At the Residence of
Mrs. George Bernard
NEW YORK
THE SOCIETY OF THE FRIENDS OF MUSIC
The Society of the Friends of Music
Fourth Concert
Wednesday, February 18th at 3:30 o'clock
Ritz-Carlton
Mr. Eugène Ysaye Mr. Gabriel Ysaye
Soloists
Mr. Arnold Volpe and String Orchestra
Mr. Camille Decreus - Piano
Mr. Frank Sealy - Organ
ONATA No. 3, op. 108, (D Minor) - Brahms
For Violin and Piano
I. Allegro II. Adagio
III. Un poco presto e con sentimento IV. Presto agitato
Mr. Eugène Ysaye
Mr. Camille Decreus
ONCERT Bach
Orchestra
Allegro
THE TONKÜNSTLER SOCIETY
ESDAY, JANUARY 23D, 1906, AT 8.50 P. M.
ASSEMBLY HALL
109 EAST 22D STREET, NEAR FOURTH AVE. NEW YORK
Programme
1. SONATA FOR PIANO (A major) manuscript
I. Allegro ma non troppo
II. Andante mosso
III. Allegro appassionato
MR. EUGENE A. BERNSTEIN
INTERMISSION
2. SONGS FOR SOPRANO
(a) Unter blühenden Bäumen
Wenn mich wie eine kalte
Mendelssohn Hall
THE
Volpe Symphony Orchestra
OF NEW YORK
A. D. VOLPE, Conductor
First Concert
Tuesday Evening, Jan. 17, 1905
SOLOIST
Louis Edlin, Violinist
Programme
BEETHOVEN Symphonie No. 2, D
Adagio molto, Allegro

Programs

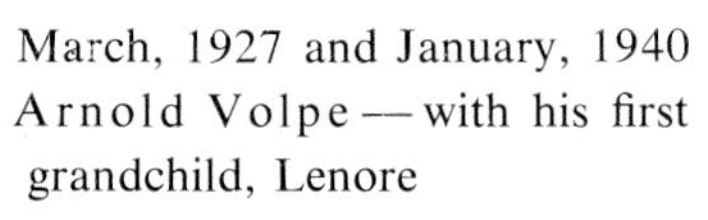

March, 1927 and January, 1940
Arnold Volpe — with his first grandchild, Lenore

Below, with his three grandchildren, Ernestine, Jerry, and Lenore

When I left for Europe, March 1914

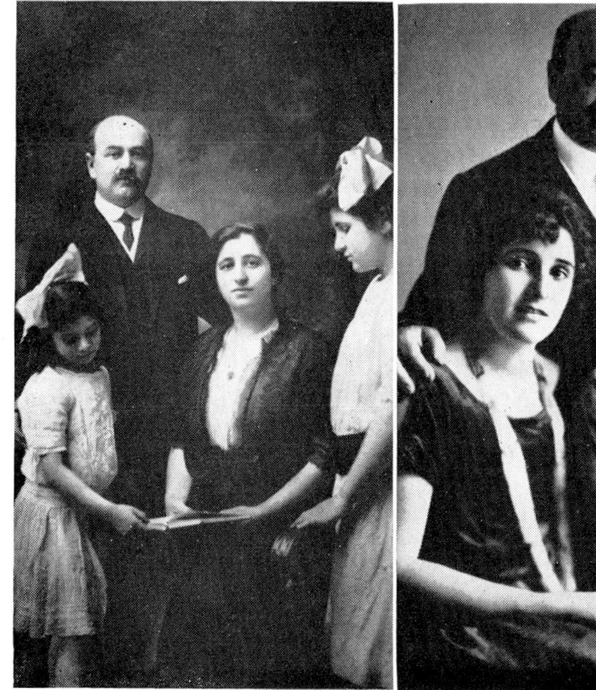

Arnold Volpe with his family, 1914

With Eleanor and Cecilia, 1922

Performance of "Faust" by Washington Opera, 1920

A picnic with the Fokines, summer of 1920. Left to right, Arnold Volpe, Mrs. L. Samoiloff, Marie Volpe, friend of Michel Fokine, Mme. Fokina, their son, Michel Fokine.

Chapter XIX

WASHINGTON OPERA—1919-1922

MANY in Washington, D.C., today are aware that the summer concerts at the Watergate on the Potomac are patterned directly after the original Stadium Concerts. In that way they connect Arnold with a contribution to the history of the Capital's cultural life.

In the constant turnover of Washington residents, not so many are aware of another earlier contribution. In the spring of 1919, when Arnold was busy with preparation for the second summer of Stadium Concerts, Eduoard Albion of Washington called on him. He told of the desire in Washington to produce operas of a high standard. He asked Arnold to come as conductor—to assemble and train chiefly local volunteer musicians for the Washington Community Opera.

The history of locally produced music in Washington has been varied. To many Europeans, one of the surprises of Washington had been that although it is the governmental capital of the United States, it never has been the major seat of artistic influence to the same extent as European capitals; not, for example, as are Paris or London.

Washington in 1919, however, was feeling an interesting renaissance, largely, perhaps, because World War I had increased its population and also given it a role of greater general prominence in the national life. With this came the question as to why Washington, as the Nation's Capital, should not become more prominent in our country's cultural life.

Among those who became deeply interested in this was Mrs. Newton D. Baker, wife of the Secretary of War. She interested Mrs. Stotesbury of Philadelphia, through whose generosity it became possible to engage Arnold as conductor of the opera.

At that time, Washington had several good legitimate theaters, but provided for music lovers nothing approaching the standards of professional opera. The Washington Community Opera had had a successful season in 1918 in the large high school, but still was unequal to the standards sought by Mr. Albion and others of like tastes and ambitions. It was fortunate that Arnold's actual work on this problem commenced in the fall of 1919, for it compelled a good part of his attention shortly after the tragedy with the Stadium Concerts committee.

The plan was to use local volunteer musicians and singers, insofar as they were available, for the operatic parts and the necessary instrumentation of the orchestra. These were the days before Washington had its own symphony orchestra.

It was the kind of challenge most conductors neither relished nor were able to meet. It was, of course, just the sort of pioneering for which Arnold was especially equipped. By many it was considered impossible. But to him it was just a stiff, healthy challenge. He plunged in, for indeed he enjoyed conducting opera as much as symphony concerts.

Mr. Albion himself was a good singer and able teacher of a large number of students. He was director-general. Charles Trier was stage director and William Van de Wall, choral director. Arnold assembled the orchestra from local musicians and commuted from New York to Washington weekly to rehearse the orchestra and chorus.

The newspapers, at least, were confident about the outcome of this putting together and training of an adequate orchestra. In the news items one could discern no inkling of the stress of the actual work involved. I quote a typical one:

"About 40 musicians, eager for the experience of playing great music under the leadership of a master conductor, assembled in Carroll Institute Wednesday night for the first orchestra rehearsal of *Faust,* conducted by Arnold Volpe of New York.

"Mr. Volpe is keen, masterful, and earnest. The men responded to his spirit and his musicianly leadership, and worked far into the night with unflagging interest.

" 'I am greatly pleased with the material,' said Mr. Volpe. 'I had not hoped to find so many good musicians in a volunteer organization. There are great possibilities here. With work, we shall have a fine orchestra.' "

The article continued:

"The personnel of the orchestra is interesting. In addition to local musicians, there are representatives from the Boston Symphony, from the Seattle Symphony, and from the Pittsburgh Symphony. Washington has become cosmopolitan, so a new era is here in musical development in the Capital."

But in the beginning, there were far fewer players with major orchestral experience than gaps in the instrumentation. To train such a group for operas was not easy. Nearly every one concerned expressed high hopes, but probably few were as confident as they were hopeful. The undertaking was tremendous.

Typical of the whole general problem I cite some of Mr. Trier's difficulties in his department and how he solved them. When Dr. Leopold Glushak, cast as Faust, was at the operating table in the surgical room of a hospital, during a rehearsal, Mr. Trier himself substituted. When Lt. Edison Davenny of the War Camps Community Service, the Mephisto, had to be absent to conduct a big community sing, Mr. Trier filled his part. When Oliver Mellum, as Valentine, was tied up in conferences with railroad magnates or government officials, Mr. Trier became the soldierly brother of Marguerite.

With conditions like this existing in all departments, the question was whether Arnold as conductor could smoothly integrate the whole, when the time came for performance.

The first presentation under Arnold's baton, *Faust,* was scheduled to begin November 17 and run for a full week at the Shubert-Garrick theater, which like most of Washington's legitimate theaters has since disappeared from the scene.

I went with Arnold to the last rehearsal. We arrived in Washington and went from the train directly to the theater. The rehearsal did not go very well. Mr. Trier was as exacting as Arnold, and the entire cast and orchestra were exhausted. At midnight, even though many parts were still ragged, some of the tired members wanted to leave. They insisted.

Arnold jumped on the stage and in a very quiet voice told them that if one person left before he was through rehearsing, there would be no performance the following night. No one left.

At the opening performance, the audience was as brilliant a sight as can be imagined. The diplomatic corps, officials, and the fashionable residential society occupied the boxes. The women in their handsome gowns and magnificent display of jewels made as delightful a scene as could be found at the opera in New York.

The performance was excellent. The Nation's Capital received it with a full measure of recognition. The press was unanimous in praise. I quote from one of the accounts of a performance later in the opening week for a note of special significance:

"With Secretary of War Baker as spokesman and a large and distinguished audience making the event Pershing Night, for General Pershing was an honor guest, *Faust* was sung by the Washington Opera Company at the Shubert-Garrick theater, and was given a delightful performance.

" 'We are here privileged to see and hear high art,' said Secretary Baker. 'But very much more than opera or play, it witnesses the achievement of permanent art in Washington, largely by Washington, and supported by Washington. So interesting it has become, in the wholly excellent performance we have enjoyed, it may be the beginning of a great artistic movement of music and art for Americans.' "

The article went on to say: "The musical and dramatic

worth of the performance was incontestable. The audience was enthusiastic. Here was *Faust* adorned with all its traditional touches, and sustained by a cast whose surety is giving an interpretation of astonishing merit."

I think the critic would have been even more astonished if he had been present at some of those early rehearsals of the volunteers.

Washington music lovers, officialdom, and society, in the way it knows how to do so well, did indeed give impressive support and appreciation. The list of opening night boxholders could have been the envy of the Metropolitan Opera House.

Our good friend, John C. Freund, editor of *Musical America,* travelled down from New York to speak at Poli's theater at the opening of the next opera, *Aida.* He had long been a champion of American musical talent. For 50 years he had labored for this cause. In the beginning, he had been almost ridiculed.

His views of this American production in the Nation's Capital were especially pointed. I quote:

"This is your opera," he said. "These are your own people. You are the people who have made it possible. Do you realize the many difficulties under which this presentation has been made? Do you realize that these people who are singing so finely before you, were rehearsing at nearly 3 o'clock this morning? Do you realize that this chorus with its fine fresh voices, these clever ballet dancers are your own?

"During the formative period of the country it was natural that we should have to rely upon Europe for our music, our art, but now the time has come when we can stand on our own feet and recognize our own talent, when it has merit, when we can make our own music, and the best, at that. The day has passed when it was necessary for our students to go to Europe, with often disastrous results.

"We Americans today lead the world in industry, in invention, in enterprise. We have produced the finest engineers, business men, doctors, lawyers, some of the finest musical instruments. In fact, in these, we today lead the world in quantity and quality. And so we shall produce out of this wondrous talent that we have among us, the finest musicians, and in time the finest music."

The article continued: "The evening passed off with the greatest éclat. It added a memorable page to the story of music in the capital. It did more; it set standards that will now be maintained, and set an example for other cities and the rest of the country to follow."

Washington was thoroughly pleased, and it was emphasized that the story would not be complete without "praise for Arnold Volpe, who conducted the opera and who, with the brief number of rehearsals permitted him, did wonders with the orchestra and the ensemble. Out of these local musicians, untrained to grand opera, he developed an organization which would have won credit even in New York."

During this period when the Washington opera was so much a part of Arnold's work, there came a brief, but dramatic, interlude. In 1921, the Musicians' Unions—Nos. 310 and 802—were on strike in New York. Needing money for the unemployed members, they announced a series of nightly benefit concerts at the Lexington Opera House and formed an orchestra of 258 musicians.

I doubt if New York ever had as large an aggregation of first-class symphony players. Until the performance began, the curtains were always closed across the stage. When they were slowly and dramatically drawn aside, it almost made one gasp to behold that great body of men—50 first violinists and other sections equally vast.

Because the performances had to be given with only one morning rehearsal, it took an experienced conductor to handle the situation. In the beginning, several conductors alternated. Before long, the only conductor was Arnold.

I recall one noon when he returned home from a strenuous

rehearsal of Tschaikowsky's *Pathetique* Symphony and Wagner's *Tannhaüser* overture. He looked very tired. I asked him why he should be the only one doing all that work—another labor of love. He looked at me in astonishment.

"Marie, you don't understand," he said. "I would not take a million dollars for the wonderful experience I had this morning. Think of it, 258 musicians playing the immortal *Pathetique*!"

What could any one say to a man whose great joy of life was to bring out the beauties of music. That evening, at the end of the symphony, the entire audience—and the orchestra—rose to their feet in acclaim. Arnold very humbly acknowledged the applause, with tears streaming down his cheeks.

The concerts were given for five weeks. A lack of adequate promotion and publicity alone prevented capacity houses. But the proceeds, I believe, were sufficient for the needs.

During the period from 1919 through 1922, Arnold conducted many operas in Washington. Some of those who took part have gone on to interesting careers. Dr. Glushak, an outstanding nose and throat specialist and plastic surgeon, went to New York, where in proof of his great feeling for music, he founded the Doctors' Orchestra.

Because the talented residents of Washington came and went, many of them with the political and administrative tides, well-known professional artists from the outside were often called to the leading parts. I particularly remember Marguerite Sylva as Carmen. I doubt if there was ever a finer Carmen. Her French diction and her portrayal of the character were superb.

For the last opera, Enrica Clay Dillon was stage director. She was a great artist in her profession.

In the four seasons of the operas there were success and pleasure and serious consideration of our continuing, until Arnold and I left the East for Kansas City.

Chapter XX

KANSAS CITY—1922-1925

JOHN A. COWAN, President of the Kansas City Conservatory of Music, came to New York in the spring of 1922 for a conference with Arnold.

He came to persuade Arnold to head the Kansas City Conservatory and to start a major symphony orchestra. At first, I did not think Arnold would accept. The picture Mr. Cowan painted was a beautiful one, though, and the salary very acceptable. The opportunities to make a real contribution to a great city's ambition to become musical center of the Middle West were enticing.

The Stadium Concerts episode still weighed heavily on Arnold, and he welcomed the idea of leaving New York for what appeared a fine challenge. Mr. Cowan explained that Arnold was to head the Conservatory as musical director. He wanted him to take personal charge of the theory department and "make it what it really should be in an institution of this kind."

But it was especially desired that Arnold organize and conduct a symphony orchestra school in the Conservatory, in which professional and non-professional musicians would be fitted for performance in a major symphony orchestra, which, it was expected, would soon be founded.

The whole summed up to an attractive full-year schedule of busy activity. A strong feature of the agreement was that when the Kansas City Symphony Orchestra should be founded, Arnold would be released from his contracted duties at the Conservatory to organize and conduct it.

In all Mr. Cowan's conversations there was revealed a civic pride and a regional ambition for musical progress that was most appealing, especially to Arnold's pioneering instincts.

Our two daughters, however, had to be considered. Eleanor had completed two years at Teachers College, Columbia University. Ceci was in her last year in high school. They would hate to leave their friends and associates in New York. Kansas City seemed a far distant place, and they had no way of knowing what the future held there.

After careful pondering, Arnold signed a contract for three years. Upon our arrival, we found a friendliness and cordiality to us personally that is a treasured memory. We were soon surrounded by a group of friends who appreciated Arnold's efforts. Among them were Mrs. Hal Gaylord, President of the Women's Auxiliary of the Conservatory—still one of my devoted friends; Hunter Gary, whose beautiful wife had a lovely contralto voice; William T. Kemper, Vice-president of the Board of Directors at the Conservatory, and Walter S. Dickey, owner of the Kansas City *Journal-Post* and Chairman of the Board of the Conservatory. It was Mr. Dickey who left in his will his large home as a foundation of the now prospering Kansas City University.

Our friend David Benjamin was one of the most beloved individuals in the community—also his sister, Fanny Benjamin. Mrs. James Neal Foster entertained generously for all our artists. Mrs. Wallace Robinson, whose husband was an owner of the Muehlbach Hotel, gave parties that could not possibly be duplicated today. Mr. and Mrs. Sig Harzfeld were our friends, although he was President of the Little Symphony, about which I shall comment later. Dr. and Mrs. B. L. Sulzbacher, Mrs. Jacob L. Loose, Mr. and Mrs. John T. Harding, and many others helped to make our stay in Kansas City more pleasant.

Arnold considered the outlook for music in Kansas City was promising. He formed within the Conservatory an orchestra which grew to a membership of 65. Three symphonic programs were given each year, and it was recognized as a fine training orchestra, preparing musicians for future orchestral careers. Arnold was anxious that the orchestra perform the same musical function as his Young Men's Symphony Orchestra in New York. He conducted it according to his firm belief that young players need, not only training on their instruments individually, but also in ensemble playing as well.

He always insisted that such an orchestra was a necessary basis for the development of music in a community, and of course the years have proved this to be true.

While we lived in Kansas City, many of our musical friends, passing through from East or West, would visit us. Usually the telegram preceding arrival would say: "Have a poker game ready" or "Have a quartet," depending on preference.

At formal affairs, however, kindred souls gathered to hear visiting artists. For example, a gala dinner was given for Ossip Gabrilowitsch, who came as conductor of the Detroit Symphony Orchestra.

Enthusiasts in the artistic advancement of the community gathered in his honor at the Bellerive hotel. The hostesses, as was the custom so often, were the officers of the Women's Auxiliary of the Conservatory. At the head table with Gabrilowitsch were Mr. Dickey, Mr. and Mrs. Cowan, Mrs. Gaylord, Mr. and Mrs. Harzfeld, Mr. and Mrs. Clifford Jones, Mrs. Loose, Miss Louise Dickey, Miss Erna Rubinstein, solo violinist with the Detroit orchestra, and her mother, Arnold and I.

Arnold presided and in one of the best speeches I ever heard him make, introduced his old friend. As a nostalgic note, too, I recall Arnold paid glowing tribute to a talented young woman encouraged by Kansas City—Miss Marion Talley—before she left for New York.

Furthering the objective of developing a long-continuing interest in fine music in the city, Gabrilowitsch conducted an afternoon concert for nearly 9,000 children in Convention Hall, as well as the evening concert.

Many other receptions were sponsored from time to time by the Conservatory, at which Arnold in his official capacity as musical director received the visiting celebrities. Rosa Ponselle, Rudolph Ganz and Fritz Reiner were among the first of a long list. With our surrounding circle of good friends, so interested and active in music for the community, and with the frequent visits of our friends from the East, we were by no means isolated from the kind of life we enjoyed.

But the anticipated creation of a major symphony orchestra did not develop—not at that time. Arnold had been promised that this would be done, and the promises were made in perfectly good faith. But in 1922, there already existed a Little Symphony Orchestra, with its own adherents. Of this we had not known until we arrived.

Many obstacles and contentions delayed establishment of a major symphony orchestra. In these clashes, Arnold already had been defeated before we appeared. In his honest efforts for the development of music, he was always the pure artist, and neither "politics" nor anything else could persuade him to lower his standards.

During our tenure of three years, he was recognized for his sound work. His instruction at the Conservatory and his training orchestra were successful. In addition, he formed equally successful chamber music trios and quartets, in which he himself played.

He had the love and respect of the entire community. But since the establishment of a full symphony orchestra was impossible in Kansas City at that time, Arnold resigned from the Conservatory in the spring of 1925.

During our stay in Kansas City, our elder daughter, Eleanor, was married. Arnold insisted we were going back to New York, which we did with our younger daughter, Ceci, by way of a summer in Hollywood, California. At the Hollywood Bowl Concerts we had a box at our disposal every evening, and it was fine meeting our old New York friends—Modest Altschuler, William C. de Mille, Ernest Bloch and many others.

One of the many letters received by Arnold on his resignation follows:

HARDING, MURPHY & TUCKER

December 20, 1924

LAW OFFICES
831 SCARRITT BUILDING
KANSAS CITY, MO.

Mr. Arnold Volpe,
Bellerive Hotel
Kansas City, Missouri.

My dear Mr. Volpe:

I am very, very sorry to know that you and your beautiful and capable wife are not going to remain here. I know somewhat of the obstacles that have been thrown in your way, but I have been hoping all the time that your splendid capacity and the great need for you here would cause these obstacles to disappear.

Kansas City needs you both very much and if we are ever going to make progress along your line of art, we must have you or such as you, and they are hard to find. I regret to have it said that our fine town, which so very much needs treatment, was unable to hold you and I am just wondering if there is anything that can be said or done that would bring about your remaining here. If so, I shall do what I can to contribute to that end.

I know there are many others who feel as I do on this subject.

Very sincerely,
John T. Harding

When we returned to New York in the fall, we leased a nice apartment and settled down. But destiny had other plans for us. Alfred Human, then connected with the publication *Musical America,* urged Arnold to accept the position at the Chicago Musical College vacated by Alexander Borowsky. Telegrams began to fly back and forth between Carl D. Kinsey, Manager of the College, and Arnold who, in the beginning, was not enthusiastic. But each succeeding message from Mr. Kinsey was more attractive. Arnold went to Chicago and signed a five-year contract. I stayed on in New York to sublease the apartment and rearrange our plans.

When I arrived, Arnold was already unhappy. He explained

he was expected to teach composition to students who did not yet know even a correct scale. To him, theory, harmony, counterpoint, and composition were almost sacred subjects.

All that year, he was much depressed. Although I urged him to go to Mr. Kinsey, who held him in high esteem, and ask for release from the contract, he struggled through the year without comment. But, when at graduation time he was faced with signing composers' diplomas for students who were not ready for them, he refused.

Then, with much humility, he went to Mr. Kinsey and poured out his heart. Mr. Kinsey's response was beautiful. He said: "Why Volpe, I respect you too much to have you unhappy. What is it you want me to do? Do you wish me to cancel your contract?" And so, as good friends, this was done.

Arnold called me on the phone and said: "Marie, I am free again! I am free again!"

For a moment, I had to hold myself. Free, but for what undertaking? None was in sight. We had never been like this before. However, our faith in our Heavenly Father helped us to face what we considered a grave difficulty.

And, of course, this was the year 1926, a year remarkable in the history of the United States for great economic developments, and a year of sanguine outlook.

Chapter XXI
SOUTHBOUND—1926

WE STARTED for the University of Miami in Coral Gables, Florida—in this way.

The day after the cancellation of the contract with the Chicago Musical College, an old friend, Benjamin Friedman, telephoned just to say hello, he said, and ask how Arnold liked his work. In a jubilant voice, Arnold told him: "I am through here. I am going back to New York, and no one can make me leave there again."

Mr. Friedman's equally jubilant response was: "I have a marvelous opportunity for you. That's what I really had in mind. Volpe, come and see me at once."

He was our good friend, and the friend, too, of many young musicians, especially violinists. He had been a good amateur violinist himself and had helped many others by paying tuitions and giving them violins. In Mr. and Mrs. Friedman's home we had spent some of our happiest hours. On New Year's Eve, for instance, with Paul Kochansky, Joseph Schwartz, Mme. Shoen Rene, Mme. Florence Easton, and others, we had dismissed all worldly cares, played games, and made music together as no concert hall ever heard it. Yes, we should listen to Mr. Friedman.

He told us he had just returned from Florida, where a great university, underwritten by nine millions of dollars, was planned for Coral Gables, a beautiful community contiguous to the City of Miami.

He had been asked by Miss Bertha Foster, he explained, to find just the man to form a major symphony orchestra, who would take charge of the violin department at the University's School of Music and help establish a chamber music department.

"I told Miss Foster, of course, there was but one man who could do that—Arnold Volpe," Mr. Friedman said.

"Friedman, save your breath," replied Arnold. "I am through doing pioneer work. I am going back to New York—and nowhere else."

But Mr. Friedman had not played all his cards. He had Miss Foster come to Chicago at his expense. She came in May 1926 and with her able charm gave a most glorious picture of the proposed University of Miami, its campus, the cottages where the faculty would live, the opportunity to do a big thing for music. Arnold succumbed to that astute presentation, to the extent of a contract for one year. He refused to sign for longer. We were to be at the opening of the University in September.

During the summer in New York, as we prepared for our trip South, Arnold was honored by an invitation to conduct two gala concerts in honor of Queen Marie of Rumania. The first of these magnificent events took place in the auditorium of the Sesqui-Centennial International Exposition in Philadelphia, on October 21; the second was given in the Metropolitan Opera House in New York, on October 24. Accordingly, we had obtained permission to postpone our arrival in Miami until October 27.

We had never been much aware of the Florida real estate boom personally, except in terms of Miss Foster's explanation of the plans for the University. Of the real estate crash and of the hurricane which had struck, we had read while we were still in New York.

The picture that confronted us on our arrival was far from the one Bertha Foster had given us. A big boat resting in the center of Biscayne Boulevard, tossed there by the storm, was mute proof of its strength. All about us, of course, we saw bewildering damage and debris, and heard endless discussions of the real estate crash. We knew things had changed since Miss Foster had been in Chicago, but we didn't know how this would affect us. We soon found that some of the men who had subscribed millions to the new University of Miami now didn't have enough money for carfare.

The great plans had exploded with the boom and vanished, for the time being, in the vortex of the hurricane.

The University of Miami had started building on 250 acres of land. Everything had to be stopped. There seemed to be nothing left but dogged determination—but an admirable sufficiency of that. So determined were those interested, especially George E. Merrick, founder of Coral Gables, that it was decided to open its doors, nevertheless. An unfinished hotel building was leased and reconstructed for the beginning of the University. Every one thought it would be temporary.

Among those who had worked tirelessly before the crash for the establishment of an orchestra were Mana-Zucca and Irvin Cassel, president of a special committee. Miss Foster was vice president and the members included:

Mrs. George E. Merrick, Dr. Bowman F. Ashe, Mrs. Thomas W. Hutson, Col. J. F. O'Leary, Daniel Cromer, Dr. William McKibben, Ernest Cotton, Judge William E. Walsh, Telfair Knight and Earl R. Billings.

At a meeting December 20, 1926, these members decided that the $70,000 in pledges was not enough to warrant undertaking a major symphony orchestra then. Besides, there were hardly any experienced musicians living in Miami at the time.

The old pioneer spirit rose again in Arnold. He went to Dr. Bowman F. Ashe, just elected first President of the University, with a suggestion.

He would call on all available musicians—students, amateurs and professionals in the community to start a volunteer orchestra.

A student member of this first group, David Alan, now a successful Miami businessman, described their first meeting:

Above, Kansas City Symphony Orchestra, 1931

At left, Arnold Volpe, receiving honorary degree of Doctor of Music from Dr. Moissaye Boguslawski, president of the Boguslawski College of Music, Kansas City, June 18, 1932.

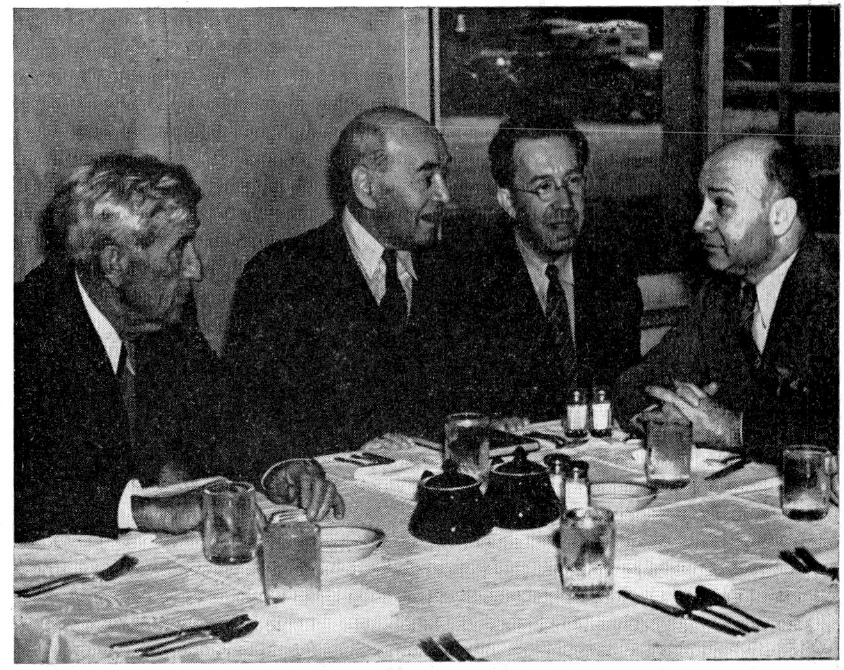

A luncheon at the University of Miami before rehearsal. Left to right, Franklin Harris, Arnold Volpe, Joel Belov, Mischa Elman

Tea at home of the Arthur Brisbanes. Left to right, Rosina Ihevinne, Josef Ihevinne, Arthur Brisbane, Mrs. Brisbane, Arnold Volpe, Mrs. Volpe

In the Fall of 1926, the first year of the founding of the University of Miami, Dr. Arnold Volpe issued a call for applicants for the symphony orchestra to be known as the University of Miami Symphony Orchestra. For the first time in the history of south Florida, a concerted effort was to be made to produce full symphony music.

Dr. Volpe called the group to order and addressed them briefly: "Ladies and gentlemen, . . . I want to welcome you to this first assembly for the University of Miami Symphony Orchestra. This is an auspicious moment—the founding of a Symphony Orchestra. And I am aware of the historical significance of this meeting of a group of musicians who will create thru their efforts and thru their talent, an orchestra which will someday achieve wide recognition as a cultural milestone in the growth of the University of Miami and indeed all of south Florida.

"The importance of this meeting is recognized by our President of the University, and he has informed me that he will be present personally, also to welcome you. I expect him in 30 minutes and as I would like to be able to welcome him as a functioning orchestra, we will rehearse immediately and prepare, in 30 minutes, something which we can play for Dr. Ashe's entrance into this room."

The rehearsal was begun. Each musician pored over his music hurriedly. Dr. Volpe raised his baton and with the experience of countless days of conducting, brought order out of nothing. Music out of sound. Symphony out of music. In 30 minutes of rehearsal the assembled group of musicians played as one, under the presence and power of the dynamic Dr. Volpe.

A knock was heard on the door—Dr. Volpe knocked his baton for attention, and called out "Come in." The door opened and Dr. Ashe, the President of the University of Miami, stepped into the room. Immediately, Dr. Volpe's baton came down on the first beat of the musical selection and the newly created orchestra played to its first audience.

Dr. Ashe stood dumbfounded. He swallowed with difficulty. His features were reflecting his amazement, his happiness, his deep emotion on finding a functioning orchestra instead of a group of unorganized musicians.

It was a poignant moment. History was in the making. Everyone in the room was aware of it. It was as if some supernatural being was present too. The music came to a halt. Dr. Volpe, smiling broadly, turned to Dr. Ashe. "Welcome, Dr. Ashe, to the University of Miami Symphony Orchestra."

Dr. Ashe, his voice filled with emotion, spoke haltingly. He tried to express his feeling on coming into a room to find an orchestra, already playing in unison and harmony. He spoke of the unison and harmony which he hoped would be possible in the future not only in the symphony orchestra which lighted the way so dramatically, but also in the whole University.

Thus, was born the University of Miami Symphony Orchestra.

In the first years, there was hardly an orchestra rehearsal Dr. Ashe did not attend. His interest in music was understanding and intelligent. A strong tie developed between the two men. They recognized in each other an indomitable will to make a success, each in his own sphere, with very little workable material. Arnold always cherished a lifelong friendship based on mutual esteem. A pioneer by instinct, he understood Dr. Ashe's problems with the whole University and held him in great admiration.

At the end of the first year the opera *Martha* was given. The entire cast, orchestra, chorus, and ballet were students of the University of Miami under Arnold's direction. The performance at the Coliseum was a great success, artistically and financially, and was a means of proving the contention of Dr. Ashe and Arnold that the finest advertising medium for an institution of learning is an emphasis on music.

There was hardly a classroom from which the sounds of music did not come forth after the usual classes were dismissed. As for me, my name for three months before the opera was changed to "Martha" Volpe. It was a tremendous undertaking at such an early date, but it was lots of fun and brought much joy and happiness to all the participants.

The orchestra grew. It took the patience of a saint and a great love of music to continue. There were daily rehearsals, and in between, as the classes changed, Arnold would stand outside his office. As the students passed by, he watched for members of the orchestra. Few escaped. He would ask: "Busy right now?"

If the answer were no, the student was soon inside practicing. During the first years, it meant even teaching some the

John Golden Theatre

202 West 58th Street • New York

Sunday Evening

NOVEMBER 17th

at 8:45 o'clock

ARNOLD VOLPE

IN A PROGRAM OF HIS COMPOSITIONS

ASSISTED BY

MARTHA ATTWOOD, *Soprano*
METROPOLITAN OPERA CO.

GEORGE MORGAN, *Baritone*

NAOUM BLINDER, *Violinist*

VLADIMIR DUBINSKY, *Violoncell*

MISHEL BERNSTEIN *Violinist* — SAMUEL STIL *Violist*

COMPOSER AT THE PIANO

(OVER)

Enclosed please find check $ for
"A Program of Compositions by ARNOLD VOLPE."
SUNDAY EVENING NOVEMBER 17TH

Name
Address

Make check
PAUL
Room 141

TICKETS

Orchestra	$2.50 and $2.00
Mezzanine	2.00
Balcony	1.50

Program

I

1. *Violoncello Soli*
   a. Meditation
   b. Chant d'Amour
   VLADIMIR DUBINSKY
2. *Songs for Baritone*
   a. Wo Ich Bin
   b. O West Wind
   c. Homeless
   d. The Burned Letter
   GEORGE MORGAN
3. *Violin Soli*
   a. Cavatina
   b. Tempo di Menuetto
   c. Mazurka
   NAOUM BLINDER
4. *Songs for Soprano*
   a. Ici-bas
   b. Thine Image, Ever in My Sight
   c. Maytime
   d. Unter Blühenden Baumen
   e. In April Weather
   MARTHA ATTWOOD

II

5. *String Quartet in G Major*
   I. Moderato Assai
   II. Allegro Scherzando
   III. Andante Cantabile
   IV. Allegro con brio

ARNOLD VOLPE *Violin*
MISHEL BERNSTEIN *Violin*
SAMUEL STILLMAN *Viola*
VLADIMIR DUBINSKY *Violoncello*

STEINWAY PIANO

An All-Volpe program, New York, November, 1929

notes. This individual instruction and group practice later brought splendid results. In the beginning, too, Arnold often went to various sections of the city, where in an hour or sometimes only a few minutes of free time available to a volunteer musician from his regular job, Arnold would sit down to teach and work with him. He made his own percussion and tympany players from wholly inexperienced men. In fact, before he was through, he had to teach almost every instrument, in order to build up a balanced ensemble.

The first concert was a revelation. No one had really believed such fine results could be obtained.

No admission was charged. Although donations were solicited and a small amount collected, the University had to carry virtually the entire burden.

In the struggling institution, there was doubt from month to month whether the faculty would be paid. But such loyalty and perseverance as were expressed by these men and women have been rarely equalled. After the first year, to reduce expenses of the University, Arnold would serve only eight months. Later it was six, then five.

I remember the distinguished columnist from Atchinson, Kansas, Edward W. Howe, who, when he was in Miami in 1930, also was writing for the Miami *Herald*. He rarely missed a concert. His interest in the progress of the orchestra was so keen he attended many of the rehearsals. Arnold was particularly proud of one of Mr. Howe's reviews, in which he compared the development of the orchestra to the building of the Panama Canal. It was by no means far-fetched.

An interested member of the orchestra was George Lowinger, amateur violist, who devoted much time to the orchestra. Another fine musician living in Miami was Jane French; hers was the first home in Miami where chamber music was played for the joy of it. She was concertmaster of the orchestra for six years. Estelle Cromer was another faithful member, also Rachel Clarke and Amelia Brod.

The orchestra grew in membership and artistry from year to year. In 1930 Arnold felt justified in inviting Nina Koshetz, the Russian soprano, to be the first soloist.

It was entirely a Russian program, which included the *Scheherazade* of Rimsky-Korsakov, and *The Burned Letter,* by Arnold Volpe. Another splendid artist who appeared that year was Naoumi Blinder, violinist. He is now the concert-master of the San Francisco Symphony Orchestra.

The orchestra also gave concerts in Palm Beach, Fort Lauderdale, Hollywood and other communities. Each concert helped prove that Florida, in spite of being called "the playground of America," is also cultural-minded.

Another tribute Arnold treasured was a letter from Mrs. Edward MacDowell, widow of the American composer.

"I am a good deal a person of impulses!" wrote Mrs. MacDowell, "and my present one is to write you a few words from an unimportant person to tell you what glowing accounts my sister, Miss Anna Nevins, brings to me of the splendid work you are doing with your orchestra.

"My sister came in yesterday, so full of enthusiasm over your work and the results and I am assuming you are like the rest of us; we can't help liking appreciation.

"I went last night to a wonderful concert with Toscanini as leader, and he is a very great one, but I can't but feel that such work as you are doing is really more important for the real spread of the love of music.

"Will you forgive, to repeat myself, an unimportant person telling you this?"

One is always tempted to describe the whole background of those early days at the University of Miami, and to explain them in terms of the whole economic situation of the Nation. But I shall allow imagination and personal recollections of the reader to fill in this background. First, there had been the real estate crash and the depression. Not only the University, as an institution, was struggling against the conditions of the depression, but the faculty and students as individuals.

For many years the orchestra rehearsed in most inadequate rooms. Under low ceilings, from which long racing boats dangled, with bad ventilation, no drinking water available, very poor instruments, and with no screens on the windows or doors, the orchestra worked at the creation of beauty and grandeur.

Most of the members were on scholarships which did not include housing or food. A great many were very poor. We would interest patrons in donating a couple of hundred dollars for food. When that was gone, we sought again. It came forth.

The one person who was "mother" to all the youngsters was "Mom Koch," Mrs. A. W. Koch. She was the kindest-hearted woman I ever met. She was in charge of the first dormitory for girls and also of distributing food to the right students. None went hungry. Among the patrons who gave often were Mrs. Lyon Krum, Mrs. H. Strongman Miller, Mrs. Alfred Mitchell, Mrs. Alice Copeland and Mrs. Henry Gregor.

Many a time Arnold would put his hand into his own pocket to feed some student, or frequently he would say: "Let's have some of the boys over for dinner." It would usually mean from ten to twenty. No matter how much I prepared, it would barely fill them up.

In those days, the faculty and the students were like one big family—yes, a jolly family, for everyone was struggling—with mutual understanding and in good spirit. It was headed sturdily by President Ashe and his good wife, sharing the little there was, and always looking toward the future with unshakable confidence and exemplary courage.

Among those we came to know and love well was the genial Franklin Harris, who joined the University staff in 1927. As the publicity director of the University, he worked with me for many years. Moreover, his gifted musicianship brought us even closer. He had studied piano and composition with some of the best-known European masters, with whom he spent many of his younger days, and he had composed beautiful songs. His love, however, for newspaper work, inherited from a newspaper family, was too strong to resist. His kindness and his consideration at the time of Arnold's passing are unforgettable.

Another good friend was George Merrick. We knew his idealism well, and were happy in furthering such magnificent vision. In his home much delightful chamber music was played.

University life was to us a new experience and an altogether exciting one. In this unique campus atmosphere, at first, were some things we did not understand. Neither of us, for instance, had ever been to a football game. The fun we had learning to appreciate it!

But there were other things more impressive. Here we saw men and women of kindred ideals sacrificing for objectives, laboring altruistically for fulfillment of noble dreams. We found, both in the community and within the University itself, taste and determination in the building of an institution, destined, we felt certain, to serve education and the cause of fine music—on a high plane.

In this there was work for us—and satisfaction. The results were the more satisfying because they were recognized—and in so many ways. As an expression to Arnold, in 1929, the people of Miami gave him a beautiful sedan at the final concert of the season.

Rufus Steele, of the *Christian Science Monitor,* presented it with this speech:

"For three perfect seasons, while the University of Miami Symphony Orchestra has swung back the portals, we have knelt in marble halls to receive our heritage from the master composers of all time. For three seasons, skipping from country to far country, we have listened to the universal language of harmony which Volpe's magic baton could make us understand. We have danced with Mozart, mourned with Tschaikowsky, marched majestically with Wagner and triumphed with Beethoven. And so, with hearts quickening and overflowing, we come to say a measureless thank-you and a fond *au revoir* until we gather here again at the opening of the fourth season in the fall.

"To Dr. Arnold Volpe, on behalf of all of us out there and others far beyond these walls, I have to say: We thank you as our virtuoso, we thank you as our maestro, but most, we thank you as our friend.

"We do not wish you to go away from us, Dr. Volpe, even for the summer, but if you and Mrs. Volpe must do that, then these, your friends on both sides of the footlights, could never suffer you to go except in state.

"You have long held the key to our hearts, and now here is the key to a glistening new automobile. It is of the genus Auburn; it is of the species sedan; but as to its sex I am not informed. The new car stands at the door of this building. When the concert is over we ask you and Mrs. Volpe to step out and climb into your chariot. Let us see how you handle a wheel—or stay—perhaps in a domestic matter like an automobile it is Mrs. Volpe who handles the wheel while you, like many a husband, will merely ride. We know Mrs. Volpe's capability, for has it not been largely her earnest work that has made these concerts so great a success?

"In any event, half the city will be out there presently to see which of you gives the magic touch that sets the motor to playing. Think, man, how you are honored! Did you ever hear that Verdi or Rubinstein or even the imperious Wagner cavorted about in his own automobile? No, no, no!

"It is a wonderful car, this Auburn sedan, and it had to be spacious so that behind the seat where you and Mrs. Volpe will sit, there might be room for that bulky baggage of our gratitude and affection and good wishes which must go with you wherever you steer.

"It is a beautiful car your friends are giving you, Dr. Volpe, but not quite the most beautiful thing, I believe, which comes from them to you. For, after all, their finest gift to you is this: They would have you know, as often as you think of them, that

'They carry your music full many a day
Long after its strains have passed away.'

"This key, in the name of you all, I present to dear Arnold Volpe, our friend."

What a fine and generous expression from the people of Miami! What an excellent car it was, too. A short time after we received it, we both learned to drive. However, it was very noticeable after rehearsals or other strenuous mental work that Arnold's mind was not at all on the wheel. To ride with him was a great strain on the nerves of everyone. Our friends urged me not to let him drive any more. So I asked him to let me be his chauffeur. At first he resented it. Nevertheless, he let me take over.

One of Arnold's most loving "pat-on-the-back" expressions to me for many years was "Just another experience." It fitted in most aptly on many occasions. Not long after we had received the car, we took a trip to Kansas City. I knew little enough about a car, and having learned to drive in flat Florida, became panicky at the thought of going over the high mountains. I told Arnold: "I don't believe I can do it. We had better get someone to drive for us."

His answer: "Of course you can do it, dear. Just another experience." After that, whenever I hesitated before some problem, it was always "Just another experience."

For eleven years we travelled only by car, taking many long trips—to New York, Rochester, Boston, Kansas City and other places. Arnold usually carried the Bible and other books to read to me aloud as I drove, or we sang hymns. Those trips ended for me after he was gone. Together they were marvelous. Alone, impossible.

Chapter XXII

SHOALS AHEAD—1931

WHEN INSTITUTIONS and individuals all over the United States were having depression troubles, in 1931, the University of Miami also faced a serious financial situation. Dr. Ashe asked Arnold and others to take a leave of absence until the University could work out its problems.

We decided to go to Kansas City, where both our daughters were living. We thought it would be nice to spend the year near them. It was three years, however, before Dr. Ashe was able to ask Arnold to return to the University.

During this leave of absence, Arnold plunged into numerous local Kansas City activities. He organized the Volpe String Quartet, consisting of himself, first violin; Turney Gibson, second violin; Carroll W. Cole, viola; and Catherine Wellemeyer, 'cello. A series of morning concerts was given for two years at the Hotel Bellerive. Membership was limited to 100, with some invited guests, and a luncheon followed each concert. The programs of the classics, as well as some modern works, were much appreciated by the press and by serious-minded music lovers.

Arnold was invited by the Y.M.H.A. and the Y.W.H.A. to organize a chorus among their members, who had expressed a great desire to learn to sing together. They called the group the Halévy Choral Society, and it consisted of men and women occupied during the day, who had never studied music. In fact, some could not read music.

Arnold taught them many of the beautiful old Russian and Hebrew compositions, among others, and the enthusiasm of the singers and their willingness to attend almost nightly rehearsals compensated for the many hours he gave them.

How very sad all these splendid young people were at the farewell reception they gave Arnold before we returned to Florida.

During the first year of this sojourn in Kansas City, an unusual request came. The Union Musicians asked Arnold to organize a symphony orchestra. The Little Symphony Orchestra had disbanded by now, and Kansas City, with all its wealth and its talent, was musically dead. Arnold's deep sympathy for the musicians made him forget all that had been thrown in the way of forming a major symphony orchestra a few years before, when he had been musical director of the Conservatory.

Through the help of our son-in-law, Jerome Joffee, the interest of Conrad Mann, President of the Chamber of Commerce, and some of the business men, was enlisted. Many others of importance, however, did not even want to listen to the proposal of a permanent symphony orchestra. They doubted if there were enough capable musicians in the city, or enough public interest.

They were "through" helping musicians. If the musicians had something to offer, let them show it. Yes, this was indeed the "Show me" state.

After many conferences, held mainly at our home, Arnold and the president and the secretary of the union met the proposition. They offered the Chamber of Commerce the services of Arnold as conductor and the services of ninety musicians in a demonstration orchestra. They would perform two concerts to prove what they had to offer. It was a tremendous undertaking. Arnold worked every day—and far into the nights—for six weeks to ready the organization for the crucial tests. They were entitled "Two Demonstration Symphony Concerts" and were set for December 17 and 18, 1931, in Convention Hall.

During the weeks before the performances, the city was much aroused. Editorial writers of the newspapers carefully aimed their typewriters and opened fire—pro and con, in and out—a spirited discussion. The news columns quoted many opinions of many community leaders. The concerts, therefore, were clearly understood to be a double-barrelled demonstration to answer two questions:

What could the orchestra be expected to do, if it were put on a permanent basis? Was there a sufficiently interested public of music lovers to support the symphony concerts in the future?

At the conclusion of the second concert, the orchestra very colorfully expressed its regard for Arnold. As a complete surprise to him, it played a specially composed fanfare. This tribute from the musicians themselves gave him much pleasure.

The audiences on both nights were enthusiastic. I quote a newspaper account of the reaction:

"Conrad Mann, who personally shouldered the financial responsibility for the two concerts, stood in his box and was greeted with the same warmth and enthusiasm shown for the music. . . .

"Applause was emphatic and prolonged following each number, and the audience rose to display its approval of Charles F. Horner's suggestion that now that Kansas City has a symphony orchestra, the City keep it."

Affirmative recognition of all that had been done and confirmation of the truth of Arnold's predictions were told in an editorial soon after the demonstration. It said:

"Those two symphony concerts were remarkable in several respects. When Arnold Volpe suggested the experiment, few persons supposed that he would find enough material in Kansas City to form a full-sized symphony orchestra. But he did not have to import a single player.

"Some persons, at least, wondered whether, even if the musicians were available, Mr. Volpe would be able to weld them into an orchestra competent to play symphonic music in a few weeks, and without the stimulus of any financial return. For it was part of his plan that he and the entire orchestra should give their services without charge. Here again he succeeded beyond all reasonable expectation.

"Finally, there must have been the question in some minds as to whether Kansas City and its surrounding territory could produce satisfactory audiences for full symphonic concerts. On successive nights, there were about 3,800 and 4,500 persons in Convention Hall to hear the programs.

"The demonstration could scarcely have been more successful. Certainly every effort should be made to keep the orchestra together . . . until the necessary financial arrangements can be worked out, to give this community the great asset of a regular symphony orchestra."

Thus, was the present Kansas City Symphony Orchestra launched under Arnold's baton.

As it is impossible to reprint the many letters received after those two concerts, I am including but two from Kansas City's leading citizens.

THEODORE GARY AND COMPANY

CHICAGO KANSAS CITY NEW YORK

H. L. GARY,
PRESIDENT

At Chicago, Illinois,
December 22, 1931.

Arnold Volpe, Esquire,
Kansas City, Missouri.
My dear Mr. Volpe:

During my absence, the news accounts of the two symphonic concerts by the local musicians under your direction have been read, and to be quite frank with you I got a thrill out of it and was more than pleased to know of the success of your concerts.

I know you will appreciate my inner desire and enthusiasm in rehabilitating symphonic music in Kansas City, and I know you must be getting much satisfaction out of the response and favorable comment and the interest that you have aroused in this undertaking.

I hope to have a visit with you when I am home over the holidays, and with our best wishes and the Compliments of the Season to you and yours,

Cordially yours,
Hunter L. Gary

R. B. JONES & SONS INC.

CLIFF C. JONES
PRESIDENT

Kansas City, Mo.
December 18, 1931

Mr. Arnold Volpe,
K. C. Musicians' Ass'n.,
1017 Washington St.,
Dear Mr. Volpe:

Please accept this note as an expression of my thorough enjoyment and appreciation of the wonderful concert, which you so admirably conducted last night.

This gives promise to interest the people of Kansas City in symphonic music, and I sincerely hope the ones who are behind your efforts will meet with such success that the concerts may be continued indefinitely, and that we may have a permanent Kansas City Orchestra.

Cordially yours,
Cliff Jones

Incidentally I never saw a finer group of ladies and men as that under your direction last night, and that means a lot too!

C. J.

There was contention, nevertheless, among the adherents of three tenacious factions in the community as to who, henceforth, would conduct it. One group was for Carl Busch, the splendid musician and kindly man who had conducted, many years before, an earlier Kansas City symphony orchestra.

Another group was for Arnold. Another was for the former conductor of the Little Symphony. It was planned to compromise by having each share the first year. Arnold was to begin the series.

But before rehearsals began again, Karl Krueger, who later conducted the Detroit Symphony Orchestra, stepped in and took over.

In the late summer of 1934, while he was pondering an offer to conduct the symphony orchestra of Houston, Texas, Arnold received a letter from Dr. Ashe. The University of Miami had weathered bankruptcy and now, like other sturdy American institutions in those days, was confidently starting a new era.

It was a shoestring era for the moment. Dr. Ashe said he would like Arnold to come back, for better or worse, at a much reduced salary. Simultaneously, Gabrilowitsch was urging Arnold to take the Houston offer of much more money. But I urged and begged him to accept Dr. Ashe's proposal.

There were many factors. We loved the community. But it was not so much the climate or the palm trees or the architecture along the hibiscus-lined streets that drew us. The people of Greater Miami had a hunger for and an appreciation of fine music. There had been a great many contributors to the fund for that Auburn automobile, for example, and in so many other ways, too, they had made their feelings clear.

But in the final consideration, it was chiefly the thought of being associated again with Dr. Ashe that won the decision. In September, 1934, we were happily on our way back to Coral Gables and the University of Miami. Unconfused, this institution, under Dr. Ashe, was moving toward its objectives with a cheerfulness and celerity that were magnetic.

Chapter XXIII

FINALE — 1934-1940

On our return to the University, Arnold found the material available for the orchestra had improved. Many talented young musicians had come, to work their way.

This suggested to Dr. Ashe special scholarships for young men and women musicians—not limited to a major in music. The only requirements were graduation from high school and proficiency on an instrument. This, he felt, would provide for a full-sized student orchestra. Most years, it did.

Arnold conducted a two-hour rehearsal every day: three times a week, string rehearsals; twice a week, full rehearsals; brasses and woodwinds, in between. There was no time wasted at these sessions.

It was perhaps a little frightening at first to young musicians to discover that the kindly Arnold Volpe was such a taskmaster. When work was being done, he was stern—all business. He shouted, he bore down, he seemed a driver of slaves. But he was always the gentleman. No matter how worked-up he might get at rehearsals, he never used profanity, although he might yell mercilessly and call them dumbbells.

But the results were almost incredible, and to the musicians themselves, completely gratifying. They soon understood that he worked, too, and prodigiously, and that he asked no more of his musicians than he asked and gave of himself. When rehearsals were over—then a complete change of personality. Jovial, sympathetic, affectionate. They called him "Papa" Volpe and felt that way about him.

What the young orchestra may have lacked technically was more than balanced by something so many conductors seek and need— eagerness, freshness of spirit and enthusiasm. Ar-

In Miami, 1928. Left to right, University of Miami President Bowman F. Ashe, Mrs. Alvin Schmoeger, Arnold Volpe, Miss Bertha Foster, Mrs. Volpe, Alvin Schmoeger, then president of the Musical Courier

Arnold and Marie Volpe with Mme. Nina Koshetz and Inna Rublova

With Mana-Zucca at left, and Grete Stuckgold when she appeared with the University of Miami Symphony

Arnold Volpe, conducting University of Miami Symphony

THE UNIVERSITY OF MIAMI
Cordially invites you to the
FIRST CONCERT
by
THE UNIVERSITY ORCHESTRA
under the direction of
ARNOLD VOLPE

SOLOISTS
Grace Hamilton Morrey
Helen Flanagan
Margarethe Morris

at the
UNIVERSITY AUDIT
SUNDAY AFTERNOON, MAR
AT 4 O'CLOCK

UNIVERSITY OF MIAMI SYMPHONY ORCHESTRA
ARNOLD VOLPE, Conductor

SECOND SUBSCRIPTION CONCERT
Monday, January 22, 1940 at 8 30 p m

SOLOIST
JOSEPH SZIGETI, *Violinist*

• • •

Program

1 Overture Russlan and Ludmilla — *Glinka*

2 Symphony No. 3 in A minor (Scotch) — *Mendelssohn*
- I Andante con moto
- II Vivace non troppo
- III Adagio
- IV Allegro vivacissimo

INTERMISSION

3 Concerto for Violin and Orchestra — *Beethoven*
- I Allegro ma non troppo
- II Larghetto
- III Rondo

Joseph Szigeti

First and last concert programs directed by Arnold Volpe at the Univ. of Miami nold felt no trepidation when he invited, as the first "box-office" name to appear with the orchestra, Mischa Elman.

When we met Mischa at the station, he asked about the orchestra with fear and trembling. "Remember, Arnold," he said, almost as if admonishing him against any practical jokes, "this is the first time in my life I am appearing with a student orchestra."

Arnold assured him he had nothing to fear. He said he was personally responsible to Mischa for the performance.

Elman answered: "Yes, I know you are responsible, but you must have players to work with."

After the first rehearsal, his amazement was beyond words. After the performance, he kept urging us to arrange a tour all over the country with him as soloist.

"Let every one know what you have accomplished with the material you have!" he exclaimed.

The next great artist was Josef Hofmann. He played two piano concertos with but one rehearsal. The orchestra was already rehearsing when I brought him to the auditorium. He listened and turned to me.

"Is the flutist an extra man?" he asked, meaning a professional employed especially for the occasion.

"No, one of the students."

He replied: "Unglaublich!"

I told him that many others had said: "Unbelievable!"

He asked about the first bassoon, the French horn, the oboe, the clarinet. The answer was the same. Although Hofmann was at the time Director of the Curtis Institute, he had to admit that the University of Miami Symphony Orchestra was making musical history. Later, he formally stated: "It was a most remarkable performance, a wonderful job. The orchestra is a very strong factor in the musical development, not only of Miami, but of the State of Florida."

Other great artists followed, each with amazement at what was being accomplished.

After the appearance of Florence Hartley, an artist-student of Mme. Louise Homer, Sidney Homer wrote Arnold:

"Last Monday was one of the happiest days I ever had. First I wanted Florence Hartley to make a tremendous hit, and she did! Then I wanted the orchestra to make a grand success, and they did. Finally, I wanted every one to appreciate your great conducting, and I felt that they did!

"They were deeply moved by the noble, exalted, and always passionate spirit of your interpretations. You know how profound is the meaning, the *real* meaning, of the great works you played, and I believe you should be very happy that, with the help of your inspired and determined orchestra, and Florence, you were able to bring that message to that great audience.

"They will not forget that meaning easily and are truly grateful—as we *are!* Warmest greetings from us both to you and Mrs. Volpe."

One of the notable aspects of the comparatively young University of Miami has been the rapid achievement of a position of firm esteem in the community. Many an older institution could envy this happy situation.

During the season of 1938-39 John Erskine was one of the speakers of the Institute of Literature at the University of Miami. Always interested in music, he attended one of the rehearsals of the symphony orchestra and listened to the overture to the *Meistersinger* and the first movement of the Cesar Franck Symphony. His amazement and surprise at the playing of the young and ambitious musicians was very gratifying to Arnold. There were many artists who appeared with the orchestra under him who were equally impressed with the fine work that was being done at the University of Miami. Among those were—just to quote a few:

JOSEF LHEVINNE: "The sureness, tone quality and rhythm of these youthful musicians is amazing. I believe it is the finest student orchestra I have ever heard."

MME. GUIOMAR NOVAES: "It's beautiful to hear this orchestra. There is so much youth in their playing. I should think that you residents here in Miami would be very proud of them, indeed!"

ABRAM CHASINS: "I am proud to play with the University orchestra and I feel it a privilege and an honor to be associated with it."

MME. GRETE STUECKGOLD: "I am astonished. This student group sounds to me like an assembly of artists. I know of nothing else I can compare them with but a top symphony orchestra."

ALBERT SPALDING: "I am amazed at the way they play together. There are other universities in the country doing work like this, but I think the University of Miami is one of the most notable. The flexibility and sensitivity of these young musicians can only be compared with that of a top professional group."

JOHN FINLEY WILLIAMSON, Director of Westminister Choir: "I think it is the finest student orchestra in the country. If the work you are doing here could be carried on in all sections of the country America would have her own great musicians."

Arthur Griffith, chief editorial writer of the Miami *Herald*, whose judgment of community thought is eminently astute, once remarked to Dr. Ashe that in his considered opinion the Symphony Orchestra, more than any one factor of the institution's activities, "had made the people of this community favorably conscious of their University."

With a smile, Dr. Ashe asked: "More than the football team?"

Mr. Griffith replied: "Yes, more than the football team."

Reminded of his statement recently, Mr. Griffith said: "I still stick to that opinion."

Other Miami newspaper men and women who wrote criticisms and articles on the orchestra during Arnold's conductorship were able and enthusiastic. For the Miami *Daily News* there was the late Wanda MacDowell, consistently enlightening to her readers. Mrs. Grace Stone Hall ably represented the *News* for a year in 1929-30. For the Miami *Herald* there were H. Blond Bliss, who wrote many fine articles on the orchestra; the late William Morrell, who conducted a column under the pen name of Hugh Hough, wherein he often helped the cause of good music; and Henry Cavendish, now with the Miami *Daily News,* music critic on the Miami *Herald* for a number of years. His able interpretations of fine music in the life of a progressive community were especially important in bringing the orchestra to the attention of music-lovers.

Many of the graduates of those and other years are today holding positions in the Dade County public schools as bandmasters, music supervisors, and teachers. Others are in numerous communities of the State. Many are playing in major symphony orchestras and in excellent radio network orchestras. The leaders of the University may well be proud of their foresight and of the results of the hard work.

Among the memories of those days are many delightful parties at the home of the President of the University and homes of the patrons of the orchestra. Arnold introduced the University Quartet at the home of Mr. and Mrs. Henry Salem Hubbell, the late portrait painter.

On the day they became grandparents, we were at tea with Mr. and Mrs. Arthur Brisbane. Other guests were Mr. and Mrs. Josef Lhevinne and Mr. and Mrs. Franklin Harris.

The string quartet often played at the home of Mr. and Mrs. George Merrick. What a hilarious round of stories was told by Josef Hofmann, Harold Bauer, and Arnold, as we sat at Mrs. H. Strongman Miller's dinner party in honor of Mr. Hofmann.

There was an unforgettable tea for the faculty of the University by Mrs. William Jennings Bryan. She was in a wheel chair, not able to move any part of her body, but her mind was so very keen and brilliant. With our good friend, her daughter, Mrs. Ruth Bryan Owen Rhode, we had Florida reminiscences in New York and a Danish luncheon in their Fifth Avenue home—vodka in the Danish tradition, but ginger ale for Arnold and me.

Suppers in the beautiful home of the Henry Gregors on the bay were always delightful affairs. Annually they also invited all the members of the orchestra for a supper with all the embellishments. Mrs. Gregor, a fine amateur violinist, played in the orchestra for a number of years. Henry Gregor, a well-known composer-pianist, has written exceptionally fine compositions.

Another musical home we enjoyed was that of Mr. and Mrs. George Hughes; their daughter, Mary Hughes Sayre, an admirable pianist, appeared with the orchestra. There are many pleasant memories of Mana-Zucca's hospitality and that of Mr. and Mrs. Gabriel Newburger.

Chamber music had been arranged one evening at the Newburgers' home. It was followed by a midnight supper. Afterward, when most of the guests had gone, Arnold turned to Mr. Newburger and the other players and said: "Now, Gabe, I really feel like playing." The quartet sat down again and played on for hours.

But despite all the friendships and delightful associations, despite all the triumphs with the orchestra, University life was not without its dark problems. How, for example, could we keep up the payments on Arnold's life insurance? One by one, I had to let the policies lapse. Of this, I never let him know, lest it worry him. To the financial future we had to shut our eyes.

Usually we went to New York for the summer. For several years Arnold had a few guest performances at the Stadium. Otherwise, he was never invited as a regular conductor. Throughout the years, the Stadium wound closed a bit. But the scar in his heart never completely healed. It remained the greatest tragedy of his life.

One summer, Arnold changed our usual plans. In 1935,

he decided to inaugurate the first summer "Pop" concerts on Miami Beach, six performances on a sharing basis with the orchestra. Walter Grossman, a fine 'cellist, who had been working with Arnold, was most helpful and acted as assistant conductor. Sam Murray, representative of the Ford Motor Company, aided by making the second half of each program a commercial broadcast.

The concerts were given in the beautiful garden of the Roney-Plaza Hotel. The audience sat around little tables. Not only the audience, but the press, was enthusiastic. The newspapers published many stories and expressed the hope that this would be the beginning of a continuing annual series. We held such hopes, too.

But even before the conclusion of the series, I realized that it was too much of a strain for Arnold on top of his winter's work. We therefore gave up the idea at the end of the one season.

I believe it is only a question of time, before this area will have an auditorium under cover and suitable for the development of "Pop" concerts on a large scale.

The constant change of personnel in the orchestra caused by graduations always worried Arnold. Each year it meant training a new group of students. In 1938, more than twenty students in the orchestra were graduated. This was a crisis. Arnold studied how he might replace them.

By the time we had reached New York for the summer, we had outlined a campaign designed to reach every high school in New York and the vicinity. In response to the offered scholarships came seventy applications. He personally held all these auditions for replacements. Among them he found better string players than heretofore. As a result of this strenuous recruitment, the next season began with the first full string section we had ever had—including eight 'cellos, basses, and violas. Up to then, the woodwind and brass sections were the most complete. Now the strings dominated.

Arnold had been in need of rest when we arrived in New York. During the hard winter season, he had never missed a single rehearsal. But when, instead of resting, he sought new personnel, the strain began to tell on him. He worried, too, about having no oboe player and an inexperienced flutist.

After he had completed auditions in New York, we spent a few delightful days with our good friend Mrs. H. Strongman Miller, who later in a memorial broadcast in tribute to Arnold recalled:

"While spending a week-end with me at my summer home in the North, I took them for a little walk to see one of my favorite beauty spots, where under spreading great elms a rippling brook cascades over rocks as it hurries on its musical way to the river below the hills. As we stood in that lovely place, Dr. Volpe said: 'Listen, listen to the music of that brook! Oh, if I could only stay right here. What music I could write!'

"Another day he said to me: 'You know, there is music everywhere; it is in all Nature. There are the birds, and there is music in the strong winds and again in the gentle breezes. Listen to it in the rustling leaves and the swaying grasses, in the many sounds of the insects, in the storms and gentle rains and running waters.'

"Then he quietly added: 'Music can soften and comfort sorrow and cure all broken hearts, if people will be still and listen. I think it is the Voice of God.' "

When the summer of 1939 came, he was even more in need of rest—but again held many auditions. Consequently, in the fall of 1939, his last year, he began his work in a weakened condition.

We gave our last party on our lawn in September 1939 for the orchestra. It came before the beginning of the symphony season. One hundred and fifty were present—Dr. and Mrs. Ashe, the music faculty and several friends, and the entire personnel of the orchestra. Under strings of gay electric lights, the tables were spread. Camp chairs were everywhere. Cold cuts, slaws, salads, eggs, dressings, soft drinks, candied apples on sticks, lollipops, ice cream and cake disappeared under the onslaught of youthful appetites.

Some of the players brought their instruments, and the evening ended with dancing. Through it all, Arnold watched his "boys and girls," with a kind personal word for each, as they laughed and joked with "Papa Volpe" at his last party for them.

Although after that I tried to make him rest as much as possible and give up most of his social duties, he still did not regain full strength. I would find him studying scores, when he should have been resting. He had never learned to relax and play. His only recreation seemed to be studying new scores and practicing on his violin. He had always kept up his daily practicing of at least an hour—until 1939. Scales and chords had always started his day. His patience in working out passages and phrases, repeating them by the hour, was almost unbelievable.

One day in December 1939 when he had just finished an arduous rehearsal, I went to his study. At the next concert, he was going to conduct the Tschaikowsky Fifth. He knew the work from cover to cover, yet he was at the piano with the score. I reproached him for not resting.

"Will you please tell me why you are studying the Tschaikowsky Fifth, a work you know so well and have conducted so many times?" I asked.

He looked at me in amazement. He replied: "If I can improve one phrase, is it not worth it?"

From December into February that winter, Florida had one of its freak "freezes." Arnold contracted a cold and could not throw it off. The school building containing the concert auditorium had been closed for two weeks, because of the weather. But when Joseph Szigeti, the guest artist, came to rehearse the Beethoven violin concerto, Arnold insisted on attending. The session lasted two hours. He was chilled to the bone.

The next morning, Arnold asked me to bring Szigeti to the house. There was one bar in the concerto that bothered him. When I spoke to Szigeti, he expressed surprise. He asked me to assure Arnold it had gone very well at the rehearsal, and for him not to worry about anything. Nevertheless, Arnold insisted that Szigeti come. They sat at the piano for just about five minutes. That was all it took. Arnold was satisfied.

The night of the concert, when we had finished dressing, we went into the living room, Arnold immaculate in his white tuxedo and very handsome despite his paleness. Sitting quietly, we read aloud the 23rd Psalm and the 91st and the 121st and finished with the Lord's Prayer. This had been our custom for the past twenty years—our personal prelude to Arnold's offering of music to the people.

It was his strong conviction and realization that man of himself can do nothing, and that it was the Father within him who did the work before the orchestra.

At the concert, Arnold conducted the overture, then collapsed as he left the stage. Joel Belov, his assistant, conducted the symphony that followed. I tried to take Arnold home during the intermission and almost succeeded, when Szigeti, taking up his violin, started running through some passages. Arnold stood up again.

He said: "Marie, I am all right. I will finish the concert. I am the only one who has rehearsed it and knows what Szigeti wants." I pleaded with him not to go on. There were two doctors backstage now, but none of us could restrain him. I arranged for him to have one of the high-seated chairs by the bass players, in case he needed it.

There was hardly a dry eye in the audience when he walked on stage again. He was so pale and so weak. Everyone felt it was the last time Arnold Volpe would be their conductor. I doubt if ever a finer accompaniment was given the Beethoven violin concerto.

Arnold stood during the entire first movement; little by little, he sat down on the high chair I had provided for him. Pneumonia had developed.

When he had been in bed a week, he asked me to suggest a prayer. I copied and put next to his bed the 15th verse of the 17th Psalm: "As for me, I will behold Thy face in righteousness, I shall be satisfied when I awake in Thy likeness."

He died very peacefully on February 2, 1940.

Dr. Ashe's beautiful tribute gave me much comfort, when in part, he said:

"The community has somehow sensed Mr. Volpe's reverent and spiritual attitude toward that music, and even in the hurry and thoughtlessness of the daily life of the people, they have accepted Mr. Volpe's values and his attitude toward music. I have often felt that as Mr. Volpe came to the platform to conduct, that somehow right then, the audience sensed his spiritual attitude toward it and in a sense devoted themselves to the same idea."

After Arnold's death, I received nearly a thousand telegrams and letters of condolence. From everywhere, his pupils, his friends, his colleagues expressed their affection and admiration.

Newspapers all over the country paid tribute to the "Founder of the Stadium Concerts."

Editorials in both Miami newspapers suggested an auditorium be erected on the University of Miami campus as a Volpe Memorial. A memorial building and orchestra fund was begun with a sponsoring and active organization. The music committee of the organization included: John Barbirolli, Harold Bauer, Walter Damrosch, Olin Downes, Mischa Elman, Mrs. Ossip Gabrilowitsch, Josef Hofmann, Ernest Hutcheson, Serge Koussevitsky, Leonard Liebling, Albert Spalding and Leopold Stowkowski.

In a message to contributors issued jointly by Hervey Allen and Mrs. H. Strongman Miller, they said in part: "It is impossible to evaluate in ponderous terms the all but mystical privilege, the actual spiritual benefit, which the flooding of a community with great music beautifully played may mean. It is a great boon, one to be thankful for, something which should not be permitted to perish or decline, once it has been brought into being."

The message closed by defining the Arnold Volpe Memorial Fund as "a truly noble, hence fitting and enduring monument to a great musician's name."

Funds could not be successfully solicited during World War II, but I am still hoping that the University will have the auditorium in his memory.

In the course of putting down these facts of Arnold's life, I have reviewed hundreds of newspaper and magazine clippings, carefully kept in more than a dozen bulging scrapbooks; files of documents, letters, and telegrams; scores of pictures and hundreds of concert programs.

Enshrined among them is the last thing he wrote. I saw him do it. It was just after his last rehearsal. Very tired, he was resting in bed. He said: "Marie, I am trying to think of a word. I know it very well, but can't say it. It is what I want to tell Joel Belov he must bring out—always bring out in music."

He paused a moment—wearily—then said: "Ah, I have it. I'll put it here, so I'll be sure to remember to tell him."

Then he wrote. On the table by his bed—beside the little bronze dog he had brought from Russia—he put the slip of paper bearing the word

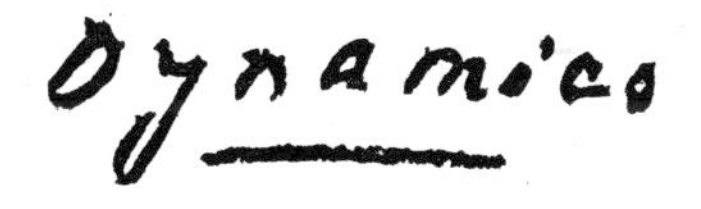

Résumé of Works by American Composers
Performed at the Lewisohn Stadium, New York

Season 1918-19

July 16	Indian Suite	*MacDowell*
	Scherzo	*Ernest Carter*
	Two Sketches - Valse Triste	*Walter Kramer*
	Chant Negre	
August 9	Suite - The Tempest	*Elliott Schenk*
	First Performance	
July 6	The Return	*Arthur Bergh*
July 7	New Russia	*Samuel Gardner*
	Repeated August 20, 1919	
July 16	Tone Poem - "Lucifer"	*Hadley*
	Angelus from Sym. No. 3	*Hadley*
	Prelude to Act III "Azora"	*Hadley*
	Ballet of the Flowers	*Hadley*
July 17	Sym. No. 4 - North, South, East, West	*Hadley*
	Ballet of the Flowers	*Hadley*
	Angelus from Symphony No. 3	*Hadley*
	Prelude to Act III "Azora"	*Hadley*
	Waltz Song - The Dance	*Hadley*
	Tone Poem - "Lucifer"	*Hadley*
August 1	Intermezzo	*James P. Dunn*
August 4	Negro Rhapsody	*John Powell*
August 6	Overture - Herod	*Hadley*
	Rhapsody - "The Culprit Fay"	*Hadley*
	Ballet of the Flowers, Suite No. 2	*Hadley*
	First Performance	
August 9	Oriental Suite - Palestine	*Platon Brounoff*
August 18	Symphony Rhapsodie in F Minor	*Walter Kramer*
August 20	Suite from Opera - Promise of Meda	*G. Aldo Randegger*
	Poem Erotique	*MacDowell*
	Scotch Poem	*MacDowell*
	Peter Pan (Scherzo)	*Frank E. Ward*
	Piano Concerto	*Mana Zucca*
	Played by Composer	
	Second Violin Concerto	*Cecil Burleigh*
	Act II "Azora"	*Hadley*
September 1	Act III "Azora"	*Hadley*
August 26	Ballet of the Flowers - Suite No. 3	*Hadley*
	First Performance	

Résumé of the Major Works performed at the Lewisohn Stadium, Season 1919.

BACH
Prelude, Choral and Fugue

BEETHOVEN
Symphony No. 5 and 7
Overture "Leonore"
Overture "Egmont"

BERLIOZ
Overture "Carnaval Romain"
Overture "Benvenuto Cellini"
March "Damnation de Faust"

BRAHMS
Symphony No. 2 and 4

BRUCH
Violin Concerto in G Minor

CHABRIER
"España"

CHARPENTIER
Impressions d' Italie

DEBUSSY
L'Apres midi d'un Faune
Fetes
Petite Suite

DE GREEF
Three Belgium Folk Songs

DELIBES
Suite "Coppelia"
Suite "Sylvia"

DUKAS
L'Aprenti Sorcier

DVORAK
Symphony "New World"
Overture "Carneval"

ENESCO
Roumanian Rhapsody

CESAR FRANCK
Symphony D Minor

GLAZOUNOV
Suite "Automne"

GOLDMARK
Symphony "Rustic Wedding"
Overture "Sakuntala"

GRIEG
Suite "Peer Gynt"
Piano Concerto in A Minor

HAYDN
Symphony No. 3

IPPOLITOW-IVANOW
"Caucasian Sketches"

LACOME
Suite "La Feria"

LALO
Norwegian Rhapsody

LEKEU
"Fantaisie sur deux Airs Angevins"

LISZT
Symphonic Poem "Les Preludes"
Symphonic Poem "Tasso"
Hungarian Fantasy
Piano Concerto in E Flat Major
Rhapsody No. 1, 2, 4, 6

MENDELSSOHN
Overture "Ruy Blas"
Midsummer Night's Dream
Violin Concerto in E Minor

MOUSSORGSKY
"A Night on Bald Mountain"

MOZART
Overture "Magic Flute"

NICOLAI
Overture "Merry Wives of Windsor"

RACHMANINOFF
Piano Concerto in C Minor

RIMSKY-KORSAKOV
"Scheherazade"
Capriccio Espagnol
Suite "Coq d'Or"

RUBINSTEIN
Piano Concerto in D Minor
Bal Costume

Saint-Saens
Symphonic Poem "Le Rouet d'Omphale"

Schubert
Symphony No. 7
Symphony No. 8 (Unfinished)

Sibelius
"Finlandia"

Smetana
"Vltava"
Overture "Bartered Bride"

Svendsen
Carnival in Paris

Tschaikowsky
Symphony No. 4, 5, 6
"Francesca da Rimini"
"Romeo and Juliet"
Capriccio Italien
March "Slave"
Suite "Nutcracker"
"The Sleeping Beauty"
Overture "1812"
Violin Concerto

Wagner
Overture "Tannhauser"
Overture "Rienzi"
Overture "Flying Dutchman"
Overture "Meistersingers"
Overture "Parsifal"
Prelude and Love Death "Tristan and Isolde"
Wotan's Farewell and Magic Fire Music
Prelude "Lohengrin"
Good Friday Spell
Ride of the Valkyries
Prize Song "Master Singers"
March "Tannhauser"

Weber
Overture "Oberon"
Overture "Freischutz"
Overture "Euryanthe"

Résumé of Miscellaneous Works performed at the Lewisohn Stadium, Season 1919.

Borodin
Ballet Music "Prince Igor"

Brahms
Hungarian Dances

Bruch
Kol Nidrei

Dvorak
Slavonic Dances
Humoresque

Elgar
Pomp and Circumstance

Glazounov
Valse de Concert

Gounod
"Ave Maria"
March "Queen of Sheba"
Fantasy "Faust"
Ballet music "Faust"

Herbert
American Fantasy
Al Fresco

Jarnefelt
Prelude
Berceuse

Liszt
"Dreams of Love"

Mendelssohn
Spring Song

Meyerbeer
March "Prophet"

Ponchielli
Ballet Music "Giocanda"

Rossini
Overture "William Tell"

Rubinstein
"Kamenoi Ostrow"
Valse Caprice
"Toreador et Andalouse"
Trot de Cavalerie
Ballet music "Feramors"

Sibelius
Valse Triste

Strauss
Overture "The Bat"
Waltz "Blue Danube"
Waltz "Southern Roses"
Waltz "Voices of Spring"

Tschaikowsky
Polonaise Suite No. 3
Andante Cantabile
Waltz "Eugen Onegin"

Volpe
Chant d'Amour
March "Reveille"

Waldteufel
Waltz "Estudiantina"
Waltz "Les Patineurs"
Waltz "España"
Waltz "Tout Paris"

Wolf-Ferrari
Two Intermezzi: "Jewels of the Madonna"

INDEX